Bridge: the Modern Game

also by these authors

BRIDGE AT THE TOP
by Terence Reese

THE COMPLETE BOOK OF BRIDGE
by Terence Reese and Albert Dormer

THE BRIDGE PLAYER'S ALPHABETICAL HANDBOOK
by Terence Reese and Albert Dormer

DEFEND WITH YOUR LIFE
by Terence Reese and Eddie Kantar

THE BLUE CLUB
English adaptation by Terence Reese

POKER: GAME OF SKILL
by Terence Reese and Anthony Watkins

MIRACLES OF CARD PLAY
by Terence Reese and David Bird (Gollancz)

BRIDGE
the Modern Game

TERENCE REESE and
DAVID BIRD

faber and faber

First published in 1983
by Faber and Faber Limited
3 Queen Square London WC1N 3AU
Filmset by Wilmaset Birkenhead
Printed in Great Britain by
Redwood Burn Ltd Trowbridge Wiltshire

© *Terence Reese and David Bird, 1983*

British Library Cataloguing in Publication Data

Reese, Terence
Bridge: the Modern Game
1. Contract bridge
I. Title   II. Bird, David
795.41'5   GV1282.3

ISBN 0-571-13053-4

Contents

Foreword

A few years ago Bert Dormer and I decided it was time to revise our *Bridge for Tournament Players*, which was first published in 1968 and was out of print. We soon found it was not just a matter of touching up here and there; about three-quarters of the book would need to be entirely rewritten. This was because, though we didn't realize it at the time, the 1970s were a period of transition in which many new ideas were in the process of development. We abandoned the project, and David Bird caught me in the right mood when he suggested it was time to bring some order to the multiplicity of bidding styles now floating around.

Our aim has been to choose the best and least artificial of the modern treatments and conventions. With rare exceptions (for example, the new 2NT opening) we have not attempted innovation. The chapters on play are designed for players who know the basics and are ready to move into the expert class.

These days, when players form a new partnership they need to spend hours on settling their methods, and their convention card soon resembles a window-pane covered with dead flies. By providing a comprehensive and ready-to-play system, we hope to shorten that process.

Terence Reese

Part 1
THE BIDDING

1 · Expressing a trump fit

Sometimes two hands fit perfectly and yield a surprising number of tricks. More often—or so it seems—the hands are a wretched fit, and the carefully considered bidding sequence nets a minus score.

Once a trump fit has been found, it is not always good enough to evaluate each hand individually and add the results. The partnership must try to assess the fit in the side suits. It is always a good sign if ruffs can be taken in the short trump hand; for example, when A x x x faces a singleton or doubleton in the dummy. These two hands are an excellent fit:

♠ A K J 8 4	♠ Q 10 9 5 2
♡ A 9 6 5	♡ 3
♢ 4	♢ 10 9 7 3
♣ J 8 5	♣ A K Q

A small slam in spades would be a sound proposition. If you switch East's minor suits, though, ten tricks are the limit. How can a partnership discover if their hands fit well? First, we will consider situations in which game is near.

Long-suit game tries

When a major-suit bid has been raised to the two-level, the most helpful form of game try is a bid in a new suit. There are two playable methods. You may agree to bid either the side suit with most losers or the shortest side suit. Both methods help responder to judge whether the hands fit well. Most players are accustomed to bidding the main side suit, and we shall follow this style.

South holds: ♠ A Q 10 8 6

South	West	North	East
1 ♠	No	2 ♠	No

♡ A 2
♢ J 9 5 4
♣ A 8

South bids 3 ♢, a long-suit game try. North will study his diamond holding before making a decision. Any singleton or doubleton holding will be favourable; so will trebletons with two honours, such as K Q x. North might hold either of these hands:

(1) ♠ K J 5 4   (2) ♠ K J 7 2
    ♡ 9 7 3   ♡ J 9
    ♢ 8 2   ♢ 7 6 3
    ♣ K 9 3 2   ♣ K 6 5 3

On the first hand he would bid 4 ♣, accepting the try. The doubleton in the game-try suit suggests that the hands will fit well. The second hand has a point more, but the worst possible holding in diamonds. North will sign off in 3 ♠.

South has a choice of game tries on this hand:

South holds: ♠ A J 8

South	West	North	East
1 ♡	No	2 ♡	No

♡ K 8 5 4 2
♢ K 7 3
♣ A Q

Should he bid 2 ♠ or 3 ♢? Neither is ideal. Despite the high point count, South's hand contains many losers. The best chance of game may well be 3NT, and South should indicate this by using 2NT as his game try.

It is sometimes good tactics to keep the enemy guessing with a false game try:

South	West	North	East	South holds: ♠ A 10 7 6 4
1 ♠	No	2 ♠	No	
?				

♡ K 9
♢ K J 10 3
♣ A K

Hoping to induce a favourable lead, South makes a spurious

game try of 3 ◇. He has no intention of staying short of game, of course.

When the agreed suit is a minor the question of a good fit is less important initially, since the target will usually be 3NT. Bids in a new suit will show values there:

South	West	North	East	South holds:	♠ 8 4
1 ◇	No	2 ◇	No		♡ A K 3
?					◇ A Q 9 7 2
					♣ A Q 5

South bids 2 ♡, showing that he has the suit well held. He hopes to hear 2 ♠ or 2NT.

Raising the barrage

When one side has a good fit, so does the other. If you find your fit first, it is important to stop the enemy from finding theirs.

South	West	North	East	South holds:	♠ 9 2
1 ♡	No	2 ♡	No		♡ K Q J 6 3
?					◇ A J 8 4
					♣ J 2

The battlefield is strangely quiet. In an effort to keep it that way, South should bid 3 ♡. North will realize that partner is raising the barrage on a hand on which he does not expect 2 ♡ to win the contract.

There is little point in this procedure when you hold spades.

South	West	North	East	South holds:	♠ A Q 9 7 6 4
1 ♠	No	2 ♠	No		♡ A 5
?					◇ K J 8
					♣ Q 3

South bids 3 ♠, telling partner to bid game if he has a few 'tops'.

Game tries by responder

Long-suit game tries may also be used by the responder:

South	West	North	East	North holds:	♠ K Q 8 3
1 ◇	No	1 ♠	No		♡ 8 5 3
2 ♠	No	?			◇ Q 4
					♣ A 10 9 7

North bids 3 ♣, showing his longest side suit. When South is minimum he will sign off now in 3 ♠ (or maybe 3 ◇). With a better hand South will bid 4 ♠—or possibly 3NT if he has a sound heart guard.

Responder can sometimes use a game try to help him choose between two possible games:

South	West	North	East	North holds:	♠ A 10 9 6
1 ♡	No	1 ♠	No		♡ K 8
2 ♠	No	?			◇ K Q J 2
					♣ J 5 4

North should not plunge into 4 ♠, maybe to find himself in a 4–3 fit. He should bid 3 ◇, showing his longest side suit. South may bid 3NT now, which will suit North's hand.

Sequences when responder is strong

A direct raise to game is a limited bid, often based on distribution. It should not be made on more than 12 points or so. Hands worth rather more than a direct game raise are covered by a sparkling array of conventions. There are so many versions of the Swiss convention, for example, that every canton seems to have its own favourite.

Super Swiss

Two types of responding hand are covered by this convention: flat hands, and those with a side-suit singleton.

1. Flat hands. Responses of 4 ♣ and 4 ◇ announce a flat hand with four-card trump support at least. The point count will be about 12–15, since stronger hands qualify for the Baron 2NT response, described in Chapter 7.

4 ♣ shows a hand with good controls (at least two aces, or one ace and the trump king). The opener may then cue-bid with a suitable hand:

		West	East
♠ K Q 9 6 4	♠ A J 8 5	1 ♠	4 ♣
♡ 3	♡ A J 7 4	4 ♢	4 ♡
♢ A Q 10 5	♢ K 8	5 ♣	5 ♢
♣ K Q 3	♣ J 9 2	6 ♠	

4 ♢ shows a sound raise to game, and little more:

		West	East
♠ A Q 4	♠ K 10	West	East
♡ K Q 10 9 6 5	♡ J 8 7 2	1 ♡	4 ♢
♢ K J 10	♢ Q 9 4 2	4 ♡	
♣ 6	♣ A Q 5		

West's hand is rich in playing strength but, warned of the lack of controls by East's 4 ♢ bid, he stops safely at the four-level.

2. Hands with a singleton. When responder has a sound raise to game, including a side-suit singleton, he makes the bid *one step beyond the double raise*:

(a) 1 ♡   3 ♠   (b) 1 ♠   3NT

In both cases the opener may request identification of the singleton by making the next available bid:

		West	East
♠ A Q J 9 5	♠ K 10 8 2	1 ♠	3NT
♡ K Q 2	♡ A J 6 4	4 ♣	4 ♢
♢ 9 7 5 2	♢ 6	4NT	5 ♠
♣ 6	♣ A J 9 3	6 ♠	

West inquires with 4 ♣ and East shows the singleton diamond. Five-ace Blackwood is wheeled out and the resultant slam is an excellent one. If East's red suits were reversed, ten tricks would be the limit of the hand. A heart singleton would carry no attraction for West; he would sign off in 4 ♠.

Note that East would show a club singleton by bidding 4 ♠. It is always possible to specify the singleton without going past game.

Minor-suit Swiss

When partner opens 1 ♣ or 1 ◇ and you have an excellent trump fit including a major-suit singleton, you make a double jump in the short suit:

				North holds:	♠ 3
South	*West*	*North*	*East*		♡ A K 6
1 ◇	No	?			◇ A Q 9 5 2
					♣ Q 10 4 3

North could bid 2 ♣, certainly, and hope to get his hand across eventually. Better is to make an immediate Swiss bid of 3 ♠, passing the message of strong trump support and a singleton spade. If partner rebids 3NT now, showing the spades well held, North is worth one more try. He will cue-bid 4 ♡, giving a clear picture of his hand.

It is true that, following this style, you lose sequences such as 1 ♣–3 ♡ to denote a pre-emptive type; but such bids are seldom useful.

Reverse Swiss

There are Swiss-type rebids as well as Swiss responses. The opener should not raise his partner directly to game if a more descriptive route is available. Sometimes he will indicate a shortage himself:

South	*West*	*North*	*East*	South holds:	♠ K Q 9 2
1 ♡	No	1 ♠	No		♡ A K J 8 2
?					◇ A 10 3
					♣ 6

South rebids 4 ♣, showing a four-card spade fit and a singleton club. Note that this call does not show *more* than a rebid of 4 ♠, which would itself be a very strong call. It shows *why* the opener's hand is worth game.

The same method applies after a two-level response:

South	West	North	East	South holds:	♠ A Q 9 5 4 2
1 ♠	No	2 ♡	No		♡ K Q 4
?					◇ 3
					♣ A 10 9

South bids 4 ◇.

Delayed game raise

When responder is worth a raise to game and has a fair side suit, he may begin by bidding his suit. This sequence suggests opening bid values and a 6-loser hand.

♠ A J 10 3 2	♠ Q 8 6 5	West	East
♡ A 9 8 2	♡ K 6	1 ♠	2 ♣
◇ K J 3	◇ 8 2	2 ♡	4 ♠
♣ 6	♣ A Q J 5 4		

West holds a fair hand with two aces, but since he has no support for partner's suit he passes 4 ♠. If East's delayed game raise had been in diamonds, West would venture 6 ♠, expecting the slam to be on a trump finesse at worst.

When the opener rebids his suit, responder may indicate a delayed game raise by cue-bidding at the four-level:

♠ A Q 9 8 5 2	♠ K 10 7 3	West	East
♡ Q 6	♡ A J 10 8 3	1 ♠	2 ♡
◇ A 7	◇ 6	2 ♠	4 ♣
♣ Q 9 5	♣ A 8 4	4 ◇	4 ♡
		6 ♠	

West's cards are working well and he has a powerful trump holding.

Game raise via a jump shift

When a delayed game raise would not tell the whole story, the response must be a jump shift:

		West	East
♠ K Q 9 6 2	♠ A 10 8 3	1 ♠	3 ♣
♡ A 6 5	♡ 10 4	3 ♠	4 ♠
◇ 10 7 2	◇ A 5	5 ♣	5 ◇
♣ K 8	♣ A Q J 9 2	6 ♠	

A game raise via a jump shift gives a strong hint that a slam is in the air. Here West has a minimum hand in terms of points, but with fair trumps, a side-suit ace, and a fitting honour in partner's suit, he is worth a further move. When East shows a diamond control, West jumps to the small slam. A fit in two suits, plus the important controls, will often produce a slam on 25 points or so.

SUMMARY

1. After 1 ♡–2 ♡ (or 1 ♠–2 ♠) a new suit by the opener is in principle a game try in a suit where he has losers.
2. When, instead, the opener bids one more of the trump suit, this is defensive (except in spades).
3. A direct raise to game is a limited bid, often based on distribution. It should not be made on more than 12 points or so.
4. *Super Swiss*. With 12–15 points, a flat hand, and four-card trump support, respond
    4 ♣ with good controls,
    4 ◇ otherwise.
   If the hand contains a side-suit singleton, bid 3 ♠ (over 1 ♡) or 3NT (over 1 ♠). The opener may make the next available bid (3NT over 3 ♠, 4 ♣ over 3NT) to discover which singleton you hold.
5. *Minor-suit Swiss*. After a minor-suit opening, a double jump in a major shows excellent trump support and a singleton in the bid major.
6. *Reverse Swiss*. Over partner's response, a jump to four in a (new) minor suit (1 ◇–1 ♡–4 ♣, for example, or

1 ♠–2 ♡–4 ◇) indicates support for responder's suit and a singleton in the minor.

7. *Delayed game raise.* When responder is worth a game raise and has a fair side suit, he should bid his suit on the first round and then jump to game. When opener rebids his suit on the second round, responder may indicate a delayed game raise by cue-bidding at the four level.

8. With an even stronger hand of this type, responder should make a jump shift on the first round.

2 · Mostly transfers

It is quite possible that systems of the future will involve opening 1 ♢ when holding a heart suit. Partner can respond 1 ♡ and then you save time by proceeding with, say, 1 ♠ or 1NT. A similar notion was exemplified in Terence Reese's frolic, the Little Major system.

While the idea has not so far been attached to opening bids, it is widely used when responding to opening bids in notrumps. Playing transfers offers considerable advantages over natural methods. Firstly, the notrump opener plays the hand, with the opening lead running up to his tenaces instead of through them. Secondly, a cascade of new bidding sequences becomes available.

For example, suppose that a 2 ♢ response to 1NT shows a heart suit and requests the opener, on all average hands, to rebid 2 ♡. Then all bids from 2 ♠ upwards can be made in two different ways—either directly on the first round of bidding or via the 2 ♢ transfer. The responder has these two ways of bidding 3NT:

(1) 1NT	3NT		(2) 1NT	2 ♢	
				2 ♡	3NT

The first sequence is a normal raise to game. The second carries the additional information that the responder holds five hearts. By giving up one natural bid, we have almost doubled the number of sequences available.

This is a typical example of transfers at work:

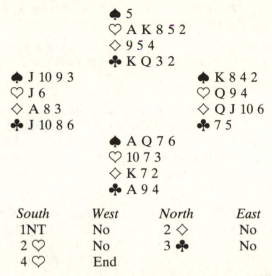

♠ 5
♡ A K 8 5 2
♢ 9 5 4
♣ K Q 3 2

♠ J 10 9 3
♡ J 6
♢ A 8 3
♣ J 10 8 6

♠ K 8 4 2
♡ Q 9 4
♢ Q J 10 6
♣ 7 5

♠ A Q 7 6
♡ 10 7 3
♢ K 7 2
♣ A 9 4

South	West	North	East
1NT	No	2 ♢	No
2 ♡	No	3 ♣	No
4 ♡	End		

North bids 2 ♢ to show his heart suit and follows with a natural game try of 3 ♣ over the 2 ♡ rebid. As South has three hearts and a fair hand he accepts the try. He should make his contract easily enough after a spade lead. Not playing transfers, North would have been the declarer and would have been killed by a diamond lead through the 1NT opener.

This is the general scheme of transfer responses to a 1NT opening:

1. 2 ♣ is initially assumed to be Stayman, but the responder may have other purposes in mind.
2. 2 ♢ shows at least five hearts; the opener will usually rebid 2 ♡.
3. 2 ♡ shows at least five spades; the opener will usually rebid 2 ♠.
4. 2 ♠ is game forcing, based on a good suit. The opener bids 2NT, after which the responder shows his suit.
5. 2NT indicates a minor-suit hand. The opener must bid 3 ♣.

6. 3 ♣ and 3 ♢ are game tries, based on a fair six-card suit.
7. 3 ♡ and 3 ♠ are pre-emptive—a long suit in a weak hand.
8. 4 ♣ and 4 ♢ are South African Texas.

Let's see how each of the responses is used. We assume a 12–14 notrump, but the principles apply to any range.

1. Stayman sequences

A response of 2 ♣, as always, asks the opener to call a major suit if he has one. With both majors he bids 2 ♡; with neither he bids 2 ♢. In some sequences the 2 ♣ bid acts as a relay, rather like a transfer, giving a different meaning to the responder's next bid. If the responder follows Stayman with two of a suit, this is always a sign-off.

(a) 1NT   2 ♣   Responder holds: ♠ Q 9 6 5 2
     2 ♢   2 ♠   ♡ J 8 7 2
                                         ♢ Q 3
                                         ♣ 9 4

The opener has no say in the matter. He must pass now.

(b) Transfer bids are not used on very weak hands, but the responder can often solve his problem with a Stayman sequence. The responses to 1NT on these three hands indicate the procedure:

(i)   ♠ K 9 7 6 2   (ii) ♠ J 2   (iii) ♠ J 7 6
      ♡ 7 3   ♡ K 10 8 5 4   ♡ Q 10 6 5 2
      ♢ Q 8 5 4   ♢ J 9 6 3   ♢ 7
      ♣ 10 8   ♣ 5 2   ♣ K 9 8 3

On the first hand you can bid Stayman and sign off in 2 ♠ over partner's response. Stayman is no use on the second hand, though, since a 2 ♠ response would leave you stranded. It is advisable to pass 1NT. Prospects are better on the third hand. If partner bids 2 ♢ you can sign off in 2 ♡; if he bids 2 ♠, you can play there.

(c) 1NT   2 ♣   Responder holds: ♠ A J 5
     2 ♡   2NT   ♡ K 6
                                          ◇ K 10 9 3
                                          ♣ 10 8 5 2

The responder does not indicate a spade suit here. Remember that 2NT on the first round would be a transfer, so this sequence is the only way to express a raise to 2NT.

(d) 1NT   2 ♣   Responder holds: ♠ A Q 5 2
     2 ♡   3 ♣   ♡ A 4
                                          ◇ 9 3
                                          ♣ K Q 9 7 4

The sequence is forcing. It shows a four-card major and at least five clubs. If the opener has a spade suit he will bid 3 ♠ now.

(e) 1NT   2 ♣   Responder holds: ♠ Q 6
     2 ♠   3 ♡   ♡ A Q J 9 5
                                          ◇ K Q 7 2
                                          ♣ A Q

Second-round bids of 3 ♡ and 3 ♠ via Stayman are similarly forcing (except when a raise of the Stayman response). They are equivalent to first-round responses of 3 ♡ and 3 ♠ in a standard system.

(f) 1NT   2 ♣   Responder holds: ♠ A J 8 5
     2 ♡   3NT   ♡ Q 8 3
                                          ◇ K 6
                                          ♣ K 10 9 4

Responder's bids here guarantee a spade suit. The opener may correct the contract if he holds four spades.

2. The 2 ◇ transfer

This shows a heart suit of at least five cards. The opener will generally rebid 2 ♡, but if he has good support for hearts he may

take another path. Look at these four 1NT openers and assume
that partner has responded with a transfer bid of 2 ◇:

(1)	(2)	(3)	(4)
♠ A Q 9 4	♠ A 10 4	♠ A J 10	♠ 10 8
♡ K 2	♡ A Q 3	♡ K 10 9 2	♡ K Q 8 3
◇ K 10 8 2	◇ K 9 4	◇ 8 5 3	◇ A 7 4
♣ Q 9 5	♣ J 10 8 2	♣ A Q 7	♣ A J 9 2

The first hand is a maximum but has a poor fit for hearts; rebid
simply 2 ♡. On the second hand opener may rebid 2NT to
indicate a maximum with three-card support of at least K x x. On
the third hand a rebid of 3 ♡ will show 4-card support and useful
values. On the last hand a rebid of 3 ♣ will give the picture of
four-card support and a fair side suit.

The responder must bear in mind that the opener may carry
the bidding to the three level. The hand must therefore be strong
enough to stand opener's more cheerful rebids. Here are some
hands that do qualify for a 2 ◇ response:

(a)	1NT	2 ◇	Responder holds:	♠ Q 6 5
	2 ♡	No		♡ K 9 8 5 3 2
				◇ 8 7
				♣ 9 2

There is no need to fear a 3 ♡ rebid on this hand. The
opponents would then have a good fit somewhere themselves.
With only five hearts and 5–3–3–2 shape, it would be better to
pass 1NT.

(b)	1NT	2 ◇	Responder holds:	♠ J 9 2
	2 ♡	2NT		♡ A J 8 4 3
				◇ Q 2
				♣ K 10 5

If the opener is minimum he may pass now or advance to 3 ♡.
Otherwise he will bid whichever game seems more promising.

(c) 1NT   2 ♢   Responder holds: ♠ 7
     2 ♡   3 ♢   ♡ K Q 7 6 5
                                        ♢ A 8 5 2
                                        ♣ Q 9 3

This sequence is forcing for one round and shows the values for a game try (at least). Opener assumes four diamonds, but responder may be simply investigating.

(d) 1NT   2 ♢   Responder holds: ♠ 9 2
     2 ♡   3 ♡   ♡ A Q 9 8 6 2
                                        ♢ A 10 3
                                        ♣ 8 5

This shows a single-suited game try, usually a six-card suit.

(e) 1NT   2 ♢   Responder holds: ♠ A J 5
     2 ♡   4NT   ♡ A J 10 8 2
                                        ♢ K 2
                                        ♣ A Q 6

4NT is a limit bid, as it would have been without the transfer. Responder shows five hearts on the way.

(f) There is one special sequence in which the 2 ♢ response does not show a heart suit:

     1NT   2 ♢   Responder holds: ♠ A Q 8 4
     2 ♡   2 ♠   ♡ 9
                                        ♢ A K 10 2
                                        ♣ K Q 6 5

This sequence initiates a Baron-style inquiry for four-card suits, usually with the intention of finding a 4–4 fit in a minor suit. The opener normally bids 2NT, after which four-card suits are bid 'upwards' until 3NT is reached or a fit is found. When the opener bids a suit directly over 2 ♠, he shows a five-card suit.

Should the opener cross responder's path by bidding other than 2 ♡ on the second round, the Baron sequence may be restored with a 3 ♠ call:

1NT	2 ♦
2NT	3 ♠

3. The 2 ♡ transfer

This shows a spade suit of five cards or more. The opener will usually rebid 2 ♠ but once again he may take stronger action with a good trump fit. The continuations after the transfer are much the same as in the previous section.

We must look here at the sequences when both majors are held:

(a) 1NT   2 ♡   Responder holds: ♠ A J 9 5 4
      2 ♠   4 ♡   ♡ A J 10 8 2
                                        ♦ Q 6
                                        ♣ 7

Responder's bids here deny slam interest. Two five-card suits are shown and the opener must choose between them.

(b) 1NT   2 ♡   Responder holds: ♠ K Q 10 5 2
      2 ♠   3 ♡   ♡ A 9 6 3
                                        ♦ Q 5
                                        ♣ 8 4

This is forcing for one round and the opener will assume a hand similar to the one shown, though responder may, of course, be stronger.

(c) Many hands that are 5–4 or 4–5 in the majors can be introduced by way of the Stayman convention already described.

4. The 2 ♠ transfer

This response serves all strong hands containing a good suit of at least six cards. The opener transfers to 2NT; then the responder reveals his suit. The opener may now bid 3NT or raise the responder's suit or show interest with a cue bid.

(a) 1NT   2 ♠   Responder holds: ♠ A Q 8
      2NT   3 ♣   ♡ A J 3
                                        ♦ 5
                                        ♣ K Q 10 7 6 2

This sequence shows a single-suiter in clubs.

(b)	1NT	2 ♠	Responder holds:	♠ A K J 8 7 2
	2NT	3 ♠		♡ A 2
				◇ K 8 3
				♣ K 7

The opener may now bid 3NT, raise to 4 ♠, or show interest with a cue bid.

5. *The 2NT transfer*

This covers most minor-suit hands. The opener is required to bid 3 ♣.

(a)	1NT	2NT	Responder holds:	♠ 3
	3 ♣			♡ J 6 5
				◇ 10 7 4
				♣ K J 9 8 6 2

This is a weakness takeout in clubs. With a similar holding in diamonds responder would bid 3 ◇ over 3 ♣.

(b)	1NT	2NT	Responder holds:	♠ K 10 2
	3 ♣	3 ♡		♡ 6
				◇ A Q J 9 3
				♣ K Q 8 7

This sequence is game-forcing, showing one or both minors and a *shortage* in hearts. If the opener is well stocked in hearts he may venture 3NT. Otherwise he must choose a minor suit, or perhaps bid 3 ♠ to indicate values in spades.

(c)	1NT	2NT	Responder holds:	♠ J 3
	3 ♣	3NT		♡ 6
				◇ A K 9 6 2
				♣ A Q 7 5 3

Here responder indicates five cards in each minor. The opener will pass only if he has both majors well under control.

6. The 3 ♣ and 3 ◇ responses

These are non-forcing game tries based on a six-card minor. The suit will always require support.

    (a) 1NT   3 ♣   Responder holds: ♠ K 6
                                                 ♡ 10 8 6
                                               ◇ Q 3
                                             ♣ A J 9 6 5 2

The opener will view favourably any hand that contains a high honour, and preferably three cards, in partner's suit.

7. The 3 ♡ and 3 ♠ responses

Jump responses in the majors are obstructive efforts which the opener must pass.

    (a) 1NT   3 ♠   Responder holds: ♠ Q 10 9 7 6 5 2
                                                 ♡ 9 6 4
                                             ◇ Q 2
                                             ♣ 8

8. The 4 ♣ and 4 ◇ responses

These are South African Texas, requesting a transfer to 4 ♡ and 4 ♠ respectively. They are used when the responder has a long suit and sees advantage in making opener the declarer.

    (a) 1NT   4 ♣   Responder holds: ♠ 6
                                                 ♡ K Q 10 9 7 6 2
                                             ◇ 8 4
                                             ♣ A 5 3

The opener will usually rebid in the indicated suit, but with good primary controls he may bid the intermediate suit, 4 ◇ in this case, to suggest slam possibilities.

Transfers opposite a 1NT overcall

The method used when partner makes a 1NT overcall is almost the same. Two clubs is Stayman and all the transfers apply (except when the suit named is the one below the opener's suit). Transfers are particularly valuable opposite a protective notrump.

South	West	North	East	West holds:	♠ 9 7 2
1 ♠	No	No	1NT		♡ K 10 9 7 3 2
No	?				◇ A 5
					♣ Q 4

West bids 2 ◇, enabling his partner to play in 2 ♡. If West were to bid 2 ♡ himself, this would be to play, from his side.

Transfers opposite a 2NT opening

When partner opens 2NT it may be important to avoid a lead through the strong hand. There is less room to manoeuvre than opposite 1NT, but the transfer scheme is similar:

1. 3 ♣ is Baron, asking opener to bid his lowest four-card suit.
2. 3 ◇ shows at least five hearts; the opener will usually rebid 3 ♡.
3. 3 ♡ shows at least five spades; the opener will usually rebid 3 ♠.
4. 3 ♠ is a transfer to 3NT.
5. 3NT indicates a minor-suit hand.
6. 4 ♣ is Gerber.
7. 4 ◇ shows a 5–6 major two-suiter.
8. 4 ♡ and 4 ♠ are to play.

We will consider these responses in turn.

1. The 3 ♣ response

After this fit-finding bid both players show their four-card suits in ascending order until 3NT is reached.

(a)	2NT	3 ♣	Responder holds:	♠ A 9 8 2
	3 ◇	3 ♡		♡ K 7 6 3
	3 ♠	4 ♠		◇ 10 4 3
				♣ 9 6

The opener has shown diamonds and spades.

  (b) 2NT   3 ♣   Responder holds: ♠ A 2
        3 ♠   4 ♣   ♡ K 10 8 3
                                        ♢ 7 5 2
                                        ♣ K Q 9 2

When the responder carries the bidding to 4 ♣, this is natural and is assumed to be a four-card suit. With no club fit the opener will sign off in 4NT.

2. *The 3 ♢ transfer*

This shows at least five hearts, as you would expect. Again the opener is free to rebid 3NT (with a maximum and three hearts) or 4 ♡ (with good trump support). Consequently the responder should not use this transfer on very weak 5–3–3–2 types.

  (a) 2NT   3 ♢   Responder holds: ♠ 9
        3 ♡   No   ♡ J 9 7 6 2
                                        ♢ 10 4 3
                                        ♣ J 8 5 4

Fearing that his hearts may pull little weight in a notrump contract, the responder aims to play in 3 ♡. If partner makes one of the strong rebids, there should be a play for game. Move one of the clubs to the spade suit, and responder should pass 2NT.

  (b) 2NT   3 ♢   Responder holds: ♠ K 3
        3 ♡   3NT   ♡ K 10 8 5 4
                                          ♢ J 9
                                        ♣ 7 6 3 2

The opener must now choose which game is the better prospect. As he will be declarer in either case, he can make an unbiased decision!

  (c) 2NT   3 ♢   Responder holds: ♠ 7 5
        3 ♡   4 ♣   ♡ A J 9 6 2
                                          ♢ 4 3
                                        ♣ K Q 8 5

Here 4 ♣ in principle shows a second suit but may also be bid on a non-existent suit such as A x x when responder wants to be sure of keeping the bidding alive.

(d) 2NT   3 ♢   Responder holds: ♠ 9 4 2
      3 ♡   4 ♡   ♡ A 10 8 5 4 2
                                           ♢ J 3
                                           ♣ 9 6

A simple hand, obviously better played by opener.

3. The 3 ♡ transfer

This bid shows at least five spades. There is only one sequence of note:

     2NT   3 ♡   Responder holds: ♠ Q 10 8 5 4
       3 ♠   4 ♡   ♡ K 9 6 5 2
                                             ♢ 7 3
                                             ♣ 3

Five hearts are shown here. With five spades and four hearts, the responder should bid 3 ♣ to look for a four-card fit. If none comes to light he must decide between 3NT and 4 ♠.

4. The 3 ♠ transfer

This bid is a transfer to 3NT and plays the same role as 2 ♠ over 1NT. In addition it is the sole means of raising 2NT to 3NT!

(a) 2NT   3 ♠   Responder holds: ♠ K 8 3
      3NT   ♡ J 7
                                             ♢ Q 10 5 2
                                             ♣ 7 6 4 3

(b) The 3 ♠ transfer is used to launch minor single-suiters and hands where the minor is accompanied by a four-card major:

     2NT   3 ♠   Responder holds: ♠ 2
      3NT   4 ♣   ♡ K Q 6 3
                                             ♢ 10 8 4
                                             ♣ A Q 9 5 2

This sequence is forcing to 4NT. The opener should introduce a major suit, if he has one, since his partner may be two-suited.

5. *The 3NT response*

The familiar sequence 2NT–3NT announces a minor two-suiter. The opener's least enthusiastic rebid is 4 ♣. With better diamonds than clubs he will rebid 4 ♢. When he has a maximum with good trump support he may rebid 4 ♡ (good clubs), 4 ♠ (good diamonds), or 4NT (good for both minors).

The opener is not allowed to pass 3NT since his partner is unlimited. The bidding may die in 4NT, though.

2NT	3NT	Responder holds:	♠ 8 3
4 ♣	4 ♢		♡ 6 5
4NT	No		♢ A J 9 8 2
			♣ K Q 7 4

6. *The Gerber 4 ♣ response*

4 ♣ is Gerber, which is occasionally useful. The opener replies according to this scheme:

4 ♢	1 ace or 4 aces
4 ♡	2 aces
4 ♠	3 aces

7. *The 4 ♢ response*

4 ♢ shows a hand with 5 spades and 6 hearts (this type is difficult to express otherwise).

2NT	4 ♢	Responder holds:	♠ K 10 8 5 2
			♡ Q 9 7 6 5 4
			♢ 6
			♣ 4

Responder may, of course, be stronger.

8. The 4 ♡ and 4 ♠ responses

Game bids in the majors are to play:

2NT	4 ♡	Responder holds:	♠ 6
			♡ J 10 8 7 6 5 2
			◇ K 9 4 3
			♣ 9

Seeing no advantage in a transfer sequence, responder bids game directly.

Transfers after 2 ♣–2 ◇–2NT

After 2 ♣–2 ◇–2NT the same kind of transfers are playable, the difference being simply that the opener is assumed to be 23–24 rather than 20–22. When the multi-coloured 2 ◇ is being played (see Chapter 11), hands of 20–22 points will be opened with a 2 ◇ bid. Transfers will then apply after 2 ◇–2 ♡–2NT or 2 ◇–2 ♠–2NT.

Continuations after 2 ♣–2 ◇–3NT

After 2 ♣–2 ◇–3NT, there is little breathing space and transfer bids are not used. The responder does not seek to improve the contract on very weak hands. These are the continuations:

(a) 4 ♣ is a Baron inquiry, forcing to 4NT or five of a trump fit;

(b) 4 ◇, 4 ♡ and 4 ♠ are all natural and forcing; the opener's least enthusiastic reaction is 4NT.

(c) 5 ♣ and 5 ◇ are to play, as in this example:

West	East	Responder holds:	♠ —
2 ♣	2 ◇		♡ 10 3
3NT	5 ♣		◇ 9 7 6 2
			♣ J 10 8 7 5 3 2

Responder's 5 ♣ bid means merely that he thinks this contract will be safer. If the opener is bristling with top cards he may advance to the slam.

SUMMARY

1. After a 1NT opening:
    (a) 2 ♣ is Stayman;
    (b) 2 ◇ shows at least five hearts;
    (c) 2 ♡ shows at least five spades;
    (d) 2 ♠ shows a strong single-suiter;
    (e) 2NT indicates a minor-suit hand;
    (f) 3 ♣ and 3 ◇ are game tries, based on a fair six-card suit;
    (g) 3 ♡ and 3 ♠ are pre-emptive;
    (h) 4 ♣ and 4 ◇ are South African Texas.
2. After a 2 ◇ or 2 ♡ response the opener may indicate a good fit by rebidding beyond two of the indicated major. Consequently, the responder should not use transfers on a minimum 5–3–3–2 type.
3. The same transfer system is used opposite a 1NT overcall, except that a response in the suit below the opener's is not a transfer.
4. After a 2NT opening:
    (a) 3 ♣ is Baron;
    (b) 3 ◇ shows at least five hearts;
    (c) 3 ♡ shows at least five spades;
    (d) 3 ♠ is a transfer to 3NT;
    (e) 3NT indicates a minor-suit hand;
    (f) 4 ♣ is Gerber;
    (g) 4 ◇ shows a 5–6 major two-suiter;
    (h) 4 ♡ and 4 ♠ are to play.
5. The same transfers are played after 2 ♣–2 ◇–2NT and, when the multi-coloured 2 ◇ is being played, after 2 ◇–2 ♡–2NT and 2◇–2 ♠–2NT.
6. After 2 ♣–2 ◇–3NT:
    (a) 4 ♣ is Baron;
    (b) 4 ◇, 4 ♡ and 4 ♠ are natural and forcing;
    (c) 5 ♣ and 5 ◇ are to play.

3 · Double!

If you study the chapter on doubles in a standard textbook, you will find a neat division between penalty and takeout doubles. Nowadays there is a third type—a double that in most situations conveys the message 'I have some values but no simple way of expressing them.'

As a result, few doubles of part-score contracts are for penalties. The double is used more often as a rapier than a bludgeon. Before describing the new wave of non-penalty doubles, we will look at the modern treatment of the takeout double.

The takeout double

Here we are on familiar ground. *When the opponents have bid one or two suits and your partner has not bid, any double of a suit bid up to the level of three is for takeout, provided it is made at the first opportunity*. All these doubles are for takeout:

	South	*West*	*North*	*East*
(a)	1 ♡	No	2 ♣	dble
(b)	1 ◇	No	3 ♣	dble
(c)	1 ♠	No	3 ♠	dble
(d)	1 ◇	No	1 ♡	No
	2 ♡	No	No	dble
(e)	2 ♡	dble	(whether 2 ♡ is weak or strong)	

When a player doubles a suit at his *second* opportunity, the double is for takeout if the opponents have found a fit (as in (d), above) and for penalties otherwise.

South	*West*	*North*	*East*
1 ♣	No	1 ♠	No
2 ♣	dble		

This is a penalty double; but if West had doubled one club on the first round, the second double would also be for takeout.

This auction is somewhat less clear:

South	West	North	East
No	No	1 ♦	No
1NT	No	2 ♦	dble

East might hold a weak takeout double of diamonds *or* be strong with diamonds. He should feel free to double with either type, trusting partner to distinguish.

A penalty pass is the equivalent of a positive bid, so here East's second double is for penalties:

South	West	North	East
1 ♦	No	No	dble
No	No	1 ♠	dble

Responding to a takeout double

The basic responses to a takeout double are well established. With a minimum hand you make a simple bid in your longest suit. With a hand of about 8–10 points you make a non-forcing jump bid. With 11 points or more, game is near; this is generally expressed by a cue bid in the opponent's suit.

Responding on a weak hand

We will look first at some of the less cheerful responding hands:

East holds: ♠ 9 6 2
♡ 8 5 3
◇ Q 7 3
♣ 10 8 6 4

(a)	South	West	North	East
	1 ◇	dble	No	?

Many players respond 1 ♡ on hands of this type, 'to keep the bidding low', as they put it. The opposite usually happens, of course. Partner, with a good fit, carries the bidding to 3 ♡, and you are in the soup tureen. It is best to respond 2 ♣ on such hands. Whatever happens then, it won't be your fault!

(b) Respond in a three-card suit only when you hold some values and no convenient alternative:

East holds: ♠ 9 3
♡ Q 10 2
♢ J 8 7 5 4
♣ K 6 5

South	West	North	East
1 ♢	dble	No	?

East bids 1 ♡. A raise of the three-card suit will not be fatal.

East holds: ♠ K J 10 2
♡ 7 4 3
♢ 9 8 4
♣ 10 7 2

(c)	South	West	North	East
	1 ♠	dble	No	?

East should borrow a point or two and bid 1NT. No great riches are promised when the opener's suit is a major.

East holds: ♠ Q 10 9 6
♡ K 8 5 2
♢ J 6 3
♣ 9 4

(d)	South	West	North	East
	1 ♠	dble	No	?

East should prefer 2 ♡ to 1NT. Partner will always be prepared for a bid in the other major, whereas a notrump response may be unwelcome.

East holds: ♠ 7 3
♡ Q J 10 8 6 5
♢ J 6
♣ Q 6 4

(e)	South	West	North	East
	1 ♡	dble	No	?

East's hearts are good enough, just, for a penalty pass. His partner is expected to lead a trump if he has one, and the aim of the defenders will be to draw trumps to prevent declarer scoring low ruffs in hand. If East's hearts were Q 10 8 x x x, he might never get the chance to draw trumps and should prefer 1NT in response to the double.

Responding on an intermediate hand

Many players bid foolishly on this type:

				East holds:	♠ A 9 7 6 4
South	*West*	*North*	*East*		♡ J 5 2
1 ♡	dble	No	?		◇ 8 2
					♣ Q 10 3

'I would have to bid 1 ♠ if my ♠ A were a small diamond,' they say, defending their jump to 2 ♠. The right test to apply in these circumstances is: Will a simple response risk missing game? This is not the case on the present hand; if partner were to raise 1 ♠ to 2 ♠, you might be worth 4 ♠, but only just.

Responding on a strong hand

When the responder has fair values but is unsure of the final denomination, he should open his account with a cue bid:

				East holds:	♠ K J 9 2
South	*West*	*North*	*East*		♡ A 10 8 2
1 ♣	dble	No	?		◇ Q 7 4
					♣ J 6

East bids 2 ♣ to show a minimum of 11 points or so. This bid is not forcing to game; it is forcing to suit agreement. If West bids two of a major, East will raise to the three level (non-forcing).

Another use for the cue bid occurs when the responder is too strong for a direct jump to game:

				East holds:	♠ A K 9 8 6 3
South	*West*	*North*	*East*		♡ Q 2
1 ♣	dble	No	?		◇ 7 6 4
					♣ A 9

A slam is possible, so East gives no thought to bidding just 4 ♠. He starts with 2 ♣ to show his strength and follows with a jump in spades on the next round.

Third hand's action over a takeout double

We turn now to the third player's action when his partner's opening bid has been doubled. The standard system for many years was to treat a simple change of suit over a double as non-forcing. It was often used as a rescue. There is little virtue in this notion because in the rare case where the fourth hand passes the takeout double for penalties, the opener knows there is a trump stack to his right. If he wishes, he may initiate a rescue himself by redoubling or trying another suit. The modern style is to play a change of suit over a double as forcing, like any other suit response.

				North holds: ♠ A Q J 6 2
South	*West*	*North*	*East*	♡ 5 4
1 ◇	dble	?		◇ A 10 4
				♣ Q 6 4

North does not waste time with a redouble. He bids 1 ♠ (forcing). The bidding will proceed as it would without the double.

				North holds: ♠ K 2
South	*West*	*North*	*East*	♡ A 10 6 4
1 ♡	dble	?		◇ 6
				♣ A Q J 9 6 4

Ignoring the double, North makes a jump shift to 3 ♣ (game forcing). He will agree hearts at a later stage, having alerted partner to slam possibilities.

				North holds: ♠ K 9 6
South	*West*	*North*	*East*	♡ 8 5 2
1 ◇	dble	?		◇ Q 7 6
				♣ Q 10 8 2

North should not pass and then wonder what to do when East's response of 1 ♡ or 1 ♠ is passed round to him. It is better to bid 1NT, showing a few pieces here and there. This will enable South to compete if he has fair playing values.

The double does make a difference when the third hand has trump support. Now he should raise to the limit:

				North holds:	♠ Q 10 8 2
South	*West*	*North*	*East*		♡ 9 6 2
1 ♠	dble	?			◇ 8 4
					♣ K J 4 2

North bids 3 ♠ in an effort to make life difficult for East. The general rule is to bid one more than you would have done without the double.

If North has a genuine raise to 3 ♠, based on points rather than distribution, he makes the conventional call of 2NT:

				North holds:	♠ K J 8 5
South	*West*	*North*	*East*		♡ 3
1 ♠	dble	?			◇ K J 7 2
					♣ Q 10 9 6

North bids 2NT, showing a sound raise to 3 ♠. This convention permits both constructive and obstructive raises to 3 ♠. 2NT is not needed in a natural sense because a balanced 11–12 count qualifies for a redouble.

The redouble

A redouble announces little support for partner and willingness in most cases to double the opponents. If the opener has a weak distributional hand, unsuitable for defence, he should declare this immediately:

				South holds:	♠ K J 10 8 6 2
South	*West*	*North*	*East*		♡ K 3 2
1 ♠	dble	redble	2 ◇		◇ 8
?					♣ K 7 3

South should rebid 2 ♠ to show a minimum opening with a long suit and little defence. With a stronger hand, still unsuitable for defence, he would pass on the second round and then remove partner's double to 2 ♠.

When the opener has a two-suited hand he should follow the same general principle, bidding at once when he is comparatively weak.

South	West	North	East	South holds:	♠ K Q 10 7 4
1 ♠	dble	redble	No		♡ 6
?					◇ A J 9 5 2
					♣ Q 2

South should bid 2 ◇ at this point. With a stronger hand he would pass for the moment and bid diamonds on the next round.

Bidding in the fourth seat

One tactical situation deserves mention:

				East holds:	♠ K 10 7 5
South	West	North	East		♡ J 7 6
1 ◇	dble	1 ♠	?		◇ 9 8 2
					♣ A 7 2

A certain type of player finds it amusing to introduce a 'schoolboy psyche' over a takeout double. North's 1 ♠ will be based on ♠ 8 x x, doubtless backed by some diamond support. To counter this, East should double on hands such as the one shown. 1NT would not be a good choice; it would show a guard in diamonds rather than in spades.

The next situation has caused much debate in expert circles:

				East holds:	♠ A 8 5
South	West	North	East		♡ K Q 9 2
1 ◇	dble	1 ♠	?		◇ 7 3
					♣ K 10 8 6

East's strength justifies a cue bid, obviously; but in which of the opponents' suits? There are two advantages in always using the opener's suit to show strength. First, it is a lower call; it allows West to rebid 2 ♡ on the above hand, for example. Secondly, East–West may wish to play in the suit introduced (spuriously, perhaps) by North. A bid in the suit bid by third hand is therefore natural:

				East holds:	♠ A Q J 8 2
South	*West*	*North*	*East*		♡ K 2
1 ◇	dble	1 ♠	?		◇ 8 5 4
					♣ 9 7 6

A double would suggest a four-card spade holding. East should bid 2 ♠, the response he would have made without North's intervention.

Responsive doubles

We turn now to other varieties of non-penalty doubles, starting with the familiar responsive double. When an opening bid is doubled for takeout and the next player raises to the two or three level, a double by the fourth player is not for penalties—it shows the values to compete but no good bid to make.

				East holds:	♠ 8 2
South	*West*	*North*	*East*		♡ K 10 4
1 ♠	dble	2 ♠	?		◇ A J 7 5
					♣ J 9 4 2

Rather than guess which minor to bid, East makes a responsive double, returning the ball to his partner's court. The fourth player will occasionally lose the chance to double for penalties, it is true, as here:

				East holds:	♠ J 5
South	*West*	*North*	*East*		♡ K J 10 7 6
1 ♡	dble	2 ♡	?		◇ Q 8
					♣ 10 7 5 2

Playing responsive doubles, East must pass. The lost penalty may return to the fold if partner reopens with a second double.

Competitive doubles

When the opponents have found a fit, it is seldom rewarding to double them for penalties at a low level. The general meaning of a double should be: 'We can probably advance in some direction, but I am not sure which direction.'

When the opponents have found a fit, a double up to the level of three is competitive.

The competitive double may be used by both sides. We look first at its use by the opening side.

South	West	North	East	South holds:	♠ K 6
1 ♣	1 ♠	2 ◇	2 ♠		♡ A Q 9 2
?					◇ J 6
					♣ A Q 7 6 5

South makes a competitive double, showing:
   (1) the values to compete;
   (2) length in the unbid suit (hearts);
   (3) some tolerance for partner's suit.

The hand would be a real puzzle if a competitive double were not available. Sometimes it is the responder who doubles:

South	West	North	East	North holds:	♠ J 6
1 ◇	1 ♠	2 ♣	2 ♠		♡ A 10 3
No	No	dble			◇ K 9 6
					♣ Q 10 8 6 5

North judges that he should not sell out to 2 ♠. Rather than pin his hopes on the diamond suit, he makes a competitive double and leaves the next move to his partner. South may choose to bid 2NT, 3 ♣, 3 ◇ or even to pass.

A special use of the bid occurs when both sides have found a fit and the opener has no room for a trial bid:

South	West	North	East	South holds:	♠ A K 8 5 4
1 ♠	2 ♡	2 ♠	3 ♡		♡ 9
?					◇ Q 8 2
					♣ A Q 9 2

South's playing strength justifies a game try, but a bid of 3 ♠ would be read as merely contesting the part score. The solution is to use a competitive double as the game try in this situation.

The defending side uses the competitive double in this type of auction:

East holds: ♠ 10 5

South	West	North	East
1 ♣	1 ♠	2 ♣	?

♡ Q 10 9 5 2
◇ A Q 8 6
♣ J 4

East doubles, showing both unbid suits well held and tolerance for partner's suit.

Until now we have considered only situations where the opponents have found a fit. There is one important use of the double where this is not the case:

South	West	North	East
1 ♡	2 ♣	2 ◇	dble

East's double is again competitive, showing a strong holding in the unbid suit (spades) and tolerance for partner's suit. These hands would qualify for such a double:

(1) ♠ Q 9 7 3 2   (2) ♠ A J 9 2
    ♡ A 8 4   ♡ Q 6 4 3
    ◇ K 5 2   ◇ A 9 5
    ♣ J 3   ♣ 10 7

Negative doubles

We move now to perhaps the most important of the new doubles—the negative or sputnik double.

A double of a suit overcall up to the level of three is a negative double. It is for takeout, requesting the opener to describe his hand further.

The negative double's major selling-point is its coverage of many previously unbiddable types:

North holds: ♠ K 10 6 5

South	West	North	East
1 ♦	2 ♣	?	

♥ Q J 7 2
♦ K 6
♣ 10 8 4

North makes a *negative double*, showing
  (1) the values to compete;
  (2) no other good bid to make.
As a rule, the doubler will have support for both the unbid suits. The opener will rebid on the initial assumption that partner holds about 7–10 points.
  A double of a major-suit overcall at the one level promises, at any rate for the moment, four cards in the other major:

South	West	North	East	South holds: ♠ 10 8 5 2
1 ♦	1 ♠	dble	No	
?				

♥ K Q 4
♦ A K J 9
♣ 6 3

Assuming that there are four hearts opposite, South rebids 2 ♥ rather than a sketchy 1NT.

North holds: ♠ K Q 2

South	West	North	East
1 ♣	1 ♦	?	

♥ J 9 6 4
♦ 8 5 4
♣ A 9 3

A double is more accurate than 1 ♥ here. Both majors are not guaranteed on this sequence.

The high-powered negative double

North faces a familiar problem on this hand:

North holds: ♠ A Q 10 8 5 2

South	West	North	East
1 ♥	2 ♣	?	

♥ 7 2
♦ J 9 5
♣ 10 3

A bid of 2 ♠ by North is normally played as forcing. He would therefore have to pass, albeit reluctantly. A welcome bounty from playing negative doubles is that North can bid 2 ♠, non-forcing, on the above hand. Partner will assume 7–10 points and a fair spade suit.

This non-forcing scheme applies only when the response is at a higher level than a simple rebid by the opener. Thus:

South	West	North	East
1 ♡	2 ◇	3 ♣	

is similarly non-forcing.

When responder wants to make a *forcing* bid in a higher ranking suit, or a suit he would have to bid at the three level, he must start with a negative double and introduce his suit on the next round:

North holds: ♠ K Q 10 8 2
♡ A 6
◇ A J 9
♣ 6 5 2

South	West	North	East
1 ♡	2 ♣	?	

North doubles. His partner will assume initially 7–10 with support for the unbid suits. When North bids spades on the next round, a new suit, the opener will readjust his sights. He will know that partner holds a *high-powered double*—a hand too good for a non-forcing suit bid on the previous round.

North holds: ♠ A Q J 9 8 6 2
♡ Q 4
◇ 2
♣ A 5 4

South	West	North	East
1 ♡	2 ◇	?	

What should North call? Two spades would be non-forcing, so should he make a high-powered double, intending to introduce his spades on the next round? This might pass off well enough, but it is better to describe the hand immediately with a jump shift to 3 ♠, forcing to game. This bid emphasizes the playing strength and avoids the slight risk that South might leave in the negative double for penalties.

South	West	North	East	North holds:	♠ A 2
1 ♠	2 ♣	dble	No		♡ A Q 10 3
2 ◇	No	?			◇ K 9 8 4
					♣ J 7 2

North's most economical advance is 2 ♡ (forcing). Since an immediate bid of 2 ♡ would have been forcing, partner will not expect five hearts when the suit is bid after a double.

All hands with one or both unbid suits can be handled with the above mechanisms. A cue bid in the overcaller's suit therefore shows a trump fit for partner and is game-forcing.

				North holds:	♠ 10 5 2
South	West	North	East		♡ A J 3
1 ◇	1 ♠	?			◇ K Q 10 6 5
					♣ K 3

North bids 2 ♠, showing a good fit in diamonds.

				North holds:	♠ 8 6
South	West	North	East		♡ K Q 9 2
1 ♣	1 ♠	?			◇ A 6 3
					♣ A J 10 4

Now North should prefer a negative double, as there may be a heart fit. If South rebids 2 ♣ or 2 ◇, North will press on with 2 ♠, forcing to game.

Playing negative doubles, what happens when a hand suitable for a penalty double arises?

				North holds:	♠ K 7
South	West	North	East		♡ 8 2
1 ♡	2 ◇	?			◇ A J 8 4 3
					♣ J 9 6 2

North must pass and hope that his partner will reopen with a double. Partnerships that play negative doubles are committed to a further attempt in most circumstances. For example, suppose that West's 2 ◇ overcall runs to South and he holds:

♠ Q J 8
♡ A Q J 5 4
♢ 7 2
♣ K 10 3

Although his hand is not far from a minimum, South should reopen with a double. The only time South may pass is when he holds length in the overcaller's suit.

SUMMARY

1. A change of suit by the third player over an opponent's takeout double is *forcing*.
2. A redouble by the third player is always penalty-oriented.
3. When the third player introduces a new suit over a takeout double, the fourth player may double (for penalties) when he has *four* cards in the suit.
4. When the fourth player holds *five* cards in the suit introduced by opener's partner, he may make a natural overcall in this suit.
5. When the third hand has bid a new suit over the takeout double, the fourth player, to show strength, must cue-bid in the *opener's* suit.
6. When the opponents have found a trump fit, all doubles up to the level of three are 'responsive' or 'competitive'. They show a desire to advance but no certainty about the best direction.
7. A double of a suit overcall up to the level of three is a *negative* (or *sputnik*) double, asking the opener to describe his hand further.
8. After an overcall, a bid by the third player above the level of two in the opener's suit is *non-forcing*. To make a forcing bid, the responder must make a negative double first and then bid the suit. This manoeuvre is known as a *high-powered* double.

9. A cue bid by the third player in the overcaller's suit shows a trump fit with the opener and is forcing to game.
10. When responder is strong in the suit of the overcall, his best way to exact a penalty is to pass and trust the opener to double. Opener does not need extra strength to do this.

4 · Forcing or not forcing?

One of the saddest ways to lose points is to pass a bid that was intended as forcing. In this chapter we look at the modern treatment of sequences that are open to misunderstanding.

Sequences when the opener rebids in notrumps

Many of the problem sequences arise when the responder's second bid is at the three level.

West	East	(E–W game)	East holds:	♠ 7
1 ◇	1 ♡			♡ K Q 9 8 2
1NT	?			◇ A J 6 5
				♣ 9 4 3

If West's rebid shows 12–14, East bids 3 ◇. This is non-forcing when the suit involved is a minor.

West	East	East holds:	♠ A Q 10 5 2
1 ♡	1 ♠		♡ K 10 5
1NT	?		◇ 6 4
			♣ K 9 7

No need to bid 3NT here. 3 ♡ is forcing and may well uncover a better game.

West	East	East holds:	♠ A K 9 6 3
1 ◇	1 ♠		♡ 7 2
1NT	?		◇ 9 5 3
			♣ A Q 10

3 ♠ at this point would be non-forcing and in any case the spades are not good enough. East could take a chance on 3NT, but 3 ♣ is better. It might elicit a preference in spades, and game in a minor suit is not excluded.

When the opener rebids 2NT, a return to his suit at the three level is forcing.

West	East	East holds:	♠ 7 2
1 ◇	1 ♡		♡ Q 9 7 6 4
2NT	3 ◇		◇ A J 8 5
			♣ 10 3

This sequence is forcing for one round at least.

Mixed sequences

A mixed sequence is one where each player supports his partner's suit. Such sequences are non-forcing when one of the suits is a minor.

West	East	East holds:	♠ 10 5
1 ◇	1 ♡		♡ K Q 8 3
2 ♡	3 ◇		◇ A 10 7 4
			♣ J 9 3

East's sequence is invitational but non-forcing. With five cards in the major, East will usually choose a different sequence. For example, if one of the spades were a small heart, he would use 3 ♣ as his game try.

West	East	East holds:	♠ K J 6
1 ♠	2 ♣		♡ J 8 5
3 ♣	3 ♠		◇ 7 2
			♣ A Q 9 8 3

Again, East's bid is non-forcing.
The situation is different when both majors are involved.

(1)	1 ♡	1 ♠	(2)	1 ♠	2 ♡
	2 ♠	3 ♡		3 ♡	3 ♠

Both these sequences are forcing, suggesting three-card support for the opener's suit.

Sequences following a one-level response

	(1)	1 ♣	1 ♠		(2)	1 ◇	1 ♠
		2 ♣	2 ♠			2 ◇	2 ♡

Sequences of this type are non-forcing but carry some weight in a constructive sense. They should not be used merely as a rescue.

West	East		East holds:	♠ K J 8 5 2
1 ◇	1 ♠			♡ Q 9 7 6 4
2 ◇	?			◇ 4
				♣ J 6

East should pass. A 2 ♡ bid has to cover many better hands not quite worth a forcing 3 ♡. It is possible, of course, to construct a hand for West where 4 ♡ would be on, but there are many more where any advance beyond 2 ◇ would lead to a minus score.

West	East		East holds:	♠ K Q J 9 6 5
1 ♣	1 ♠			♡ J 8 3
2 ♣	?			◇ A J 6
				♣ 4

East bids 3 ♠, strongly invitational and suggesting opening-bid values.

	(1)	1 ◇	1 ♠		(2)	1 ◇	1 ♠
		2 ♣	2 ♠			2 ♣	3 ♠

In the first sequence a responder with ♠ K J 10 x x x and little else may have no alternative but to rebid his suit. The 2 ♠ call is therefore less constructive than it would be facing a 2 ◇ rebid. This has a lowering effect on the 3 ♠ call, which may now be no better than ♠ A Q 10 x x x and an ace. With a stronger hand the responder must introduce the fourth suit, intending to bid 3 ♠ on the next round.

A reverse by responder is forcing for one round and is sometimes based on a three-card suit.

West	East	East holds:	♠ A Q 2
1 ♣	1 ◇		♡ 9 6
2 ♣	?		◇ A K 10 8 4
			♣ 8 5 3

East bids 2 ♠ (forcing).

When the opener makes a jump rebid of his suit, any further bid by responder below the game level is forcing.

West	East	East holds:	♠ 10 7
1 ◇	1 ♡		♡ A Q 9 8 3
3 ◇	?		◇ J 2
			♣ K 10 4 2

Unsure of the best spot, East treads water with 3 ♡ (forcing).

A reverse bid by the opener is non-forcing when the response was at the one level.

West	East	East holds:	♠ K J 8 5 4
1 ◇	1 ♠		♡ J 9 2
2 ♡	?		◇ 7
			♣ J 7 4 2

The responder may pass now. When he does bid, he has two ways of showing limited values: he may rebid his own suit, or give preference to opener's first suit at the three level.

(1)	1 ◇	1 ♠	(2)	1 ◇	1 ♠
	2 ♡	2 ♠		2 ♡	3 ◇

These sequences are non-forcing. Responder has several paths open to him when he is stronger:

(1) 1 ◇	1 ♠	(2) 1 ◇	1 ♠	(3) 1 ◇	1 ♠	(4) 1 ◇	1 ♠
2 ♡	2NT	2 ♡	3 ♣	2 ♡	3 ♡	2 ♡	3 ♠

When the final denomination is in doubt, the fourth suit may be used to extract a further call from the opener. A raise of the second suit (when the second suit is a reverse) is forcing and so is a jump rebid of responder's suit.

To play 2NT forcing after a reverse is convenient on many hands.

West	East	East holds:	♠ A 10 8 7 2
1 ◇	1 ♠		♡ J 9
2 ♡	?		◇ J 4
			♣ K 8 5 3

East bids 2NT (forcing). With ♣ K Q 9 x he would call 3NT, indicating that the fourth suit was well held but that his hand was not well constructed for a slam.

A jump shift by the opener is forcing to game over a suit response but not over 1NT.

West	East	East holds:	♠ 8 5
1 ♠	1NT		♡ 10 4
3 ♡	?		◇ K J 9 5 2
			♣ Q 10 8 6

East's hand could hardly be less suitable. He bids 3 ♠ (non-forcing). If one of the spades were a small club, he would pass 3 ♡.

Sequences following a two-level response

Here we meet a recent development: *a two-level response is forcing to 2NT*. This involves some stiffening of the requirements for a response at the two level:

		East holds:	♠ 9 3
West	East		♡ 10 2
1 ♠	?		◇ Q 8 5
			♣ A Q J 9 6 4

With a strong playable 9-count East is just worth a 2 ♣ response.

		East holds:	♠ 6 5
West	East		♡ 9
1 ♠	?		◇ Q 7 6
			♣ K J 10 7 6 4 2

Now it is probably best to pass; indeed, this represents the best chance to play eventually in 2 ♣ or 3 ♣, since the fourth player will generally reopen.

There are many situations where the 'forcing to 2NT' method leads to a gain of bidding space.

West	East	West holds:
1 ♠	2 ♢	♠ A Q 8 6 5 2
?		♡ Q 5
		♢ 7 3
		♣ A K 7

West bids simply 2 ♠ (forcing).

West	East	West holds:
1 ♡	2 ♢	♠ A 6
?		♡ K Q 9 7 6 4
		♢ A Q 5
		♣ 8 3

Again West makes a simple rebid in his suit, 2 ♡, allowing plenty of room for investigation.

West	East	West holds:
1 ♡	2 ♣	♠ 9
?		♡ K Q J 9 7 6 4
		♢ A 8 2
		♣ K 5

2 ♡ would be forcing but West prefers 3 ♡ to emphasize the quality of his suit.

West	East	West holds:
1 ♠	2 ♣	♠ A 10 9 8 3
?		♡ 10 7 5
		♢ A Q J
		♣ K 6

With such disparate holdings in the red suits West rebids 2 ♢ (forcing) rather than 2NT. This will place 3NT in the right hand if East holds, say, ♡ K x or ♡ A J.

Since a simple change of suit is forcing, a jump shift carries the message of trump support.

West	East	West holds:	♠ 4
1 ♡	2 ♣		♡ A Q J 9 5
?			◇ A K 3
			♣ K J 6 2

West rebids 3 ◇, showing good club support and a feature in diamonds. The sequence suggests a singleton in the unbid suit, spades in this instance.

After a two-level response a 2NT rebid by opener shows a minimum hand (12–14½ points).

West	East	West holds:	♠ Q 9 7 6 2
1 ♠	2 ◇		♡ A J 5
?			◇ J 4
			♣ K J 10

West rebids 2NT, more accurate than 2 ♠ with such a flimsy suit.

If your style is to play a strong notrump when vulnerable, you will now seldom need to make a prepared bid on a three-card minor.

(1)	♠ A K 8 2	(2)	♠ J 7 4 2	(3)	♠ J 9 6 4
	♡ 10 5		♡ A K 9 3		♡ K 10 4
	◇ K Q 7 6		◇ Q 10 4		◇ A K J 3
	♣ J 9 3		♣ K 3		♣ 10 3

On hand (1) you can open 1 ♠ and rebid 2NT over 2 ♡. On (2) you can open 1 ♡ and rebid 2NT over two of a minor. Similarly, hand (3) may be opened 1 ◇.

Responder takes advantage of the 'forcing to 2NT' scheme on this type.

West	East	East holds:	♠ A 8
1 ♡	2 ♣		♡ J 5
2 ◇	?		◇ Q 7 6
			♣ A J 8 4 3 2

East bids 2 ♡ (forcing), gaining time and space on an awkward hand.

After a two-level response a reverse by opener is forcing to game or to four of responder's suit.

(1)	1 ♦	2 ♣	(2)	1 ♦	2 ♣	(3)	1 ♦	2 ♣
	2 ♡	2NT		2 ♡	3 ♣		2 ♡	3 ♦

All these sequences are forcing.

After a so-called 'high reverse' (a non-jump rebid by opener at the three level) all continuations are forcing for one round.

West	East	East holds:	♠ J 9 5
1 ♡	2 ♦		♡ J 4
3 ♣	?		♦ A K 10 8 6 2
			♣ Q 7

East bids 3 ♦ (forcing); 3 ♡ would also be forcing at this point.

Sequences involving the fourth suit

'Fourth suit forcing' is such an integral part of constructive bidding that one wonders how the giants of yesteryear managed without it.

West	East	East holds:	♠ K Q 10 8 2
1 ♡	1 ♠		♡ A 5
2 ♣	?		♦ 9 7 6
			♣ A 5 4

No natural bid is remotely satisfactory. East bids 2 ♦ (the fourth suit), asking partner to describe his hand further.

A fourth-suit bid by responder at the two level is forcing for one round only.

West	East	West holds:	♠ J 7 2
1 ♦	1 ♠		♡ 5
2 ♣	2 ♡		♦ A J 9 8 2
?			♣ A K 7 5

West is well worth 3 ♠ at this point. His partner has promised around 11 points and is likely to hold five spades. Move a spade to the heart suit and the call would be 2 ♠ (non-forcing).

West	East	West holds:	♠ A Q 9 6 4
1 ♠	2 ♣		♡ K 10 5
2 ♢	2 ♡		♢ A J 9 3
?			♣ J

This example is similar. With 15 points facing a fourth-suit bid, West must bid 3NT, not a non-forcing 2NT.

When the fourth-suit bidder makes a further call at the three level, the force is continued.

West	East	East holds:	♠ K J 9 5 3
1 ♡	1 ♠		♡ J 3
2 ♣	2 ♢		♢ A 2
2 ♠	?		♣ A Q 8 4

East bids 3 ♣ (forcing). This would have been non-forcing on the previous round, of course. Following a bid of the fourth suit, it is unlimited.

When the opener raises the fourth-suit bid, he shows four cards there.

West	East	West holds:	♠ K J 9 2
1 ♢	1 ♡		♡ 6
1 ♠	2 ♣		♢ A K J 6
?			♣ A 10 7 3

West bids 3 ♣. This is forcing and promises more than a minimum hand. If the king of diamonds were a small diamond, West would rebid 2NT.

SUMMARY

1. When the opener has rebid 1NT, a jump to three in his original suit is invitational in a minor and forcing in a major.
2. When the opener has rebid 2NT, support for opener's suit at the three level by responder is forcing.
3. Mixed sequences (where each player supports his partner) are non-forcing unless both majors are involved.

4. When the opener makes a minimum rebid in his suit, the responder should normally pass on a weak hand. Any advance in his own strain is to some extent constructive.
5. A reverse bid by opener is non-forcing after a one-level response.
6. After such a non-forcing reverse, responder may show limited values by rebidding his own suit or by giving preference to opener's first suit. Any other advance (including 2NT) is forcing.
7. A reverse by responder is forcing for at least one round.
8. After a 1NT response, a jump shift by opener is non-forcing.
9. A two-level response is forcing to 2NT.
10. After a two-level response, a 2NT rebid by opener shows 12–14½ points.
11. After a two-level response, a reverse by opener is forcing to game or to four of partner's suit.
12. After a two-level response, a jump shift by opener shows strong trump support for partner.
13. At the one or two level a 'fourth suit' bid is forcing for one round only. At the three level it is forcing to game.
14. When the fourth-suit caller makes a further bid at the three level, this is forcing.
15. A raise of the fourth-suit bid shows four cards in the suit and is forcing.

5 · Pre-emptive bidding

Pre-emptive openings are notoriously difficult to counter, which is why they are made. Following the aggressive style of the modern game, players are willing to turn a blind eye to the 'Rule of 500', at any rate when not vulnerable.

Generally speaking, a hand is suitable for a pre-emptive bid when the playing strength greatly exceeds its defensive strength. Look at these examples.

(1)	(2)	(3)
♠ K Q 10 9 7 5 2	♠ A Q 9 7 6 3 2	♠ A K Q J 9 6 2
♡ 7 4	♡ 8	♡ 9 3
◇ 10 9 3	◇ K 6	◇ 10 7 2
♣ 5	♣ 10 4 2	♣ 5

Hand (1) is an obvious 3 ♠ opening, non-vulnerable. Some players we could name would risk the call even at game all. Hand (2) is unsuitable for a pre-emptive bid at any score. The suit is broken and there are two defensive high cards. 1 ♠ is the correct opening. Hand (3) is a typical 4 ♠ opening at any vulnerability.

Pre-emptive openings in the second and fourth positions should always be sound. Less discipline is required in the third seat. The weaker you are, the stronger the fourth player is likely to be. Also, since your partner is a passed hand, he will not carry you to the sky.

It used to be held that pre-empts should be avoided on shapely hands, such as 6–5–2–0. However, many good players make such bids on occasions. Without saying this is right (and perhaps encountering your scorn when it turns out badly), we won't say that it is wrong!

The 3NT opening

The Acol 3NT opening shows a solid minor suit and at most a queen outside. When responder intends to play in partner's minor, he will normally bid 4 ♣ (or 5 ♣ if prepared to play in either suit at the five level).

A response of 4 ◇ is conventional and asks opener to show a singleton:

West	East		
		♠ 3	♠ Q 10 4 2
3NT	4 ◇	♡ J 8 2	♡ A 9 7 3
4 ♠	6 ♣	◇ 7 4	◇ A K Q J
		♣ A K Q J 9 6 5	♣ 3

With no singleton, West would rebid 4NT (and East would pass). With a minor-suit singleton, the opener bids five of his trump suit.

South African Texas 4 ♣ and 4 ◇ openings

An opening 4 ♣ shows a good 4 ♡ opening with about eight playing tricks and at least one high card outside the trump suit. 4 ◇ shows a similar hand in spades. These hands would qualify for a 4 ♣ opening:

(1)	♠ J 9 3	(2)	♠ A 2
	♡ A K Q 10 8 7 2		♡ K Q 10 9 7 6 5 2
	◇ K 8		◇ 3
	♣ 6		♣ K 4

Responder can make a slam suggestion by bidding the intermediate suit (4 ◇ over 4 ♣, for example). Such a call makes no reference to the actual suit named. The opener would reject the advance on hand (1) and would cue-bid the spade ace on hand (2).

Responding to pre-empts

A new suit at the three level is natural and forcing:

		East holds:	♠ Q 3
West	*East*		♡ A Q 10 6 5 2
3 ♢	?		♢ Q 6
			♣ A K 10

East bids 3 ♡. His partner will raise on any suspicion of support, or bid 3 ♠ with a stop in that suit.

When responder bids four of a major, that is to play. Four of a minor is a cue bid.

		East holds:	♠ K Q 6
West	*East*		♡ A K 10
3 ♠	?		♢ J 5
			♣ A K J 3 2

East bids 4 ♣, hoping that his partner can show a diamond control. If he can, Blackwood will follow.

A new suit at the five level asks for a control in the suit named. It suggests that the hand is solid, bar the suit of the asking bid. The opener replies:

1st step: no control
2nd step: K or singleton
3rd step: A or void

This example shows the style:

West	*East*	♠ J 8	♠ A 10
4 ♡	5 ♣	♡ K Q J 9 8 7 6 4	♡ A 5
5 ♡	6 ♡	♢ 7 6	♢ A K Q J 5
		♣ 9	♣ J 8 4 2

The same scheme applies when the opening bid is at the three level, as in a sequence such as 3 ♠–5 ♢.

A single raise of a four-level opening carries a special meaning:

		East holds:	♠ 7
West	*East*		♡ A K Q 2
4 ♠	5 ♠		◇ A 10 9 6 5 3
			♣ A 4

East's call announces that the side suits are solid. It asks the opener to bid six if he has a one-loser trump suit. With a solid trump suit the opener bids 5NT.

When three of a major is raised to five, the message is similar—how good are your trumps?

		East holds:	♠ A Q 2
West	*East*		♡ 8 5 2
3 ♡	5 ♡		◇ A 9
			♣ A K Q 7 3

The new 2NT opening

2NT is not needed to show a balanced 20–22 count; that is covered by the multi-coloured 2 ◇, described in Chapter 11. Instead, the 2NT opening shows either a fairly strong pre-empt in diamonds, hearts or spades, including two of the top honours, or a fair minor two-suiter. These hands would qualify:

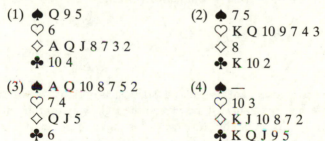

(1) ♠ Q 9 5
    ♡ 6
    ◇ A Q J 8 7 3 2
    ♣ 10 4

(2) ♠ 7 5
    ♡ K Q 10 9 7 4 3
    ◇ 8
    ♣ K 10 2

(3) ♠ A Q 10 8 7 5 2
    ♡ 7 4
    ◇ Q J 5
    ♣ 6

(4) ♠ —
    ♡ 10 3
    ◇ K J 10 8 7 2
    ♣ K Q J 9 5

Partner will normally respond 3 ♣. Opener then names his suit, or bids 3NT on the minor two-suiter.

West	East	♠ K Q 10 8 5 4 2	♠ A 6
2NT	3 ♣	♡ K 9 6	♡ A 10 3
3 ♠	4 ♠	◇ 8 2	◇ 9 7 6 4
		♣ 9	♣ K Q 8 5

East would pass a pre-emptive 3 ♠ but can raise the stronger opening, expecting to find a partner with a good card outside the trump suit.

A 3 ◇ response requests the opener to pass when he has the minor suits or just diamonds.

		East holds: ♠ K J 9 2
West	East	♡ K 10 8 7 3
2NT	?	◇ 9 6
		♣ 5 2

East bids 3 ◇, keeping the bidding low when West has the minor two-suiter and incidentally protecting his major-suit kings.

When responder has a good hand with a major-suit singleton or doubleton, and can be fairly confident that partner has this suit, he bids three of the major (forcing):

		East holds: ♠ 3
West	East	♡ A Q 3
2NT	?	◇ A K 9 6 4 2
		♣ K 7 4

East bids 3 ♠. If West holds spades, as is likely, he will raise to 4 ♠ and the hand will be played the right way up. Should West not hold spades, he must warn his partner by rebidding 3NT. Any other advance, such as 4 ♣, would be a cue bid.

Defending against pre-empts

In fourth position a double of any pre-emptive opening is based on tricks rather than strength in the enemy suit.

				East holds:	♠ A Q 8
South	*West*	*North*	*East*		♡ 7 2
4 ♡	No	No	?		◇ K Q 9 4
					♣ A K 10 2

East doubles. West will take out only when he is unbalanced and has a long suit.

In second position the meaning of a double varies according to the level of the opening:

1. Against 3 ♣ or 3 ◇: a double is primarily for takeout; 3NT is 'to play'.
2. Against 3 ♡ or 3 ♠: double implies a strong hand, with sufficient tricks to support a takeout into a long weak suit; 3NT is for takeout.
3. Against 4 ♣ or 4 ◇: double shows high cards.
4. Against 4 ♡: a double should contain tolerance for spades; 4NT is for takeout, with emphasis on the minors.
5. Against 4 ♠: a double is for penalties; 4NT is for takeout, but may be based on a two-suiter. Responder must name his lowest playable suit.

SUMMARY

1. A 3NT opening shows a solid minor suit with no more than a queen outside.
2. In response to 3NT, all club bids are to play in the opener's minor. 4 ◇ asks the opener to show a singleton; with no singleton he replies 4NT; with a minor-suit singleton he bids five of the trump suit.
3. *South African Texas*. 4 ♣ shows a good 4 ♡ opening, 4 ◇ a similar hand with spades. Responder may suggest a slam by bidding the intermediate suit.

Responding to pre-empts

4. A new suit at the three level is natural and forcing.
5. Four of a minor suit is a slam suggestion, but four of a major is to play.
6. A new-suit response at the five level asks for a control in the suit named. The opener gives a three-step reply: (1) no control (2) K or singleton (3) A or void.
7. A raise to five of the trump suit requests the opener to bid six with good trumps. If the opener has a solid trump suit he bids 5NT.

The new 2NT opening

8. An opening 2NT shows:
   (a) an upper-range pre-empt in diamonds, hearts or spades; or
   (b) a minor two-suiter.
9. Responder normally bids 3 ♣, after which the opener rebids his suit (or 3NT with the minor two-suiter).
10. A 3 ◇ response requests the opener to pass unless he has a major-suit type.
11. With a good hand and a major-suit singleton or doubleton, the responder may bid three of the short major (forcing). The game, or slam, will then be played by the right hand.

Defending against pre-empts

Normal tactics, but note:
12. Double of 4 ♡ by second hand implies tolerance for spades.
13. 4NT over 4 ♠ may be based on a two-suiter and partner should respond in a low rather than a high suit.

6 · All about overcalls

Suit overcalls, and subsequent bidding by the defenders, go almost unnoticed in some books on bidding. This is absurd, because the battle for the part score is one of the most interesting and important areas of the game. A problem arises at once from the wide range of hands covered by a suit overcall at the one level.

(1) ♠ K Q J 10 6   (2) ♠ A K J 9 6
     ♡ 9 4   ♡ 5
     ♢ 8 5 2   ♢ 10 8 6
     ♣ J 9 4   ♣ A Q 9 6

Assuming an opening bid of 1 ♢, most players would overcall 1 ♠ on the first hand, albeit somewhat guiltily if vulnerable. The bid will suggest a sound opening lead for partner and may well deter the opponents from bidding a makable 3NT. The second hand also merits a 1 ♠ overcall, the shortage in hearts precluding a takeout double.

How can the defending side bid accurately when the initial overcall covers such a wide range of hands? A well defined scheme of responses is essential. The method must allow for obstructive raises on hands with a good fit but few high cards. It must also provide constructive sequences when responder sees a chance of game.

This is a rough guide to responses when partner has overcalled at the level of one:

ACTION	STRENGTH	DESCRIPTION
Direct raises	Limited	Pre-emptive in nature
Cue bid	10+	Shows sound raise in overcaller's suit
New suit	10+	Constructive but non-forcing
Jump shift	12+	Forcing for one round
1NT 2NT 3NT	10–12 13–14 15+	Includes stop(s) in opener's suit

Note, however, that point count is less important than playing strength. For example, in a notrump contract a holding of Q J 9 x in the opponent's suit will doubtless be more effective than A x x. Another important factor is the vulnerability. A non-vulnerable overcall may be no more than a gesture; a vulnerable overcall should always promise fair values.

This is an everyday situation:

South	West	North	East
1 ♦	1 ♠	No	?

East holds: ♠ Q 10 9 3
                ♡ 8 2
                ♦ 10 7

(N–S game)
                ♣ K J 9 5 4

East should raise to 3 ♠ in an effort to shut out the opener, who is marked with a good hand. Since East raised directly, West will know that the bid was obstructive. Suppose, for example, that the bidding continues in this fashion:

South	West	North	East
1 ♦	1 ♠	No	3 ♠
dble	No	4 ♡	No
No	dble	No	?

East should not pull the double on the grounds that he has little defensive strength. He has already described his hand.

This is the other side of the coin:

South	West	North	East	East holds:	♠ A Q 7 2
1 ♣	1 ♡	No	?		♡ A 9 4
		(love all)			◇ K 10 8 5
					♣ J 6

East bids 2 ♣ to show interest in game. Remember that any direct raise, such as 3 ♡, would be pre-emptive. If his partner rebids only 2 ♡, East is clearly worth a raise to 3 ♡, but the final decision should be left to partner. When the overcall is in a major suit, partner's cue bid will usually be based on a hand with trump support. Following a minor-suit overcall, 3NT is more often the target and the cue bid's primary meaning is to request a stop in the opponent's suit.

The scheme is unchanged when the third player has joined in the auction:

South	West	North	East	East holds:	♠ A 9 6 4
1 ♡	1 ♠	2 ♡	?		♡ 10 5 2
		(N–S game)			◇ A J 9 7
					♣ K 6

East bids 3 ♡ to show a sound raise to 3 ♠ based on high-card points. South may now try an unjustified 4 ♡, hoping the opponents will take the 'automatic' sacrifice. West must not fall into the trap. Unless his playing strength suggests that 4 ♠ will make, he will be willing to defend against 4 ♡. He knows that his partner's hand contains some high cards.

South	West	North	East	East holds:	♠ 8 4
1 ◇	1 ♠	No	?		♡ A K 6
		(love all)			◇ 10 2
					♣ K Q J 8 5 2

East bids just 2 ♣—constructive but non-forcing.

South	West	North	East	East holds:	♠ A J
1 ♠	2 ◇	No	?		♡ A Q 10 7 5 2
		(E–W game)			◇ K J 7
					♣ Q 5

Any red-suit contract between 4 ♡ and 7 ♡ is a possibility. East begins with a jump-shift to 3 ♡ (forcing for the moment). If partner rebids 4 ◇, East will proceed with a cue bid of 4 ♠.

South	West	North	East	East holds:	♠ K Q 6 3
					♡ J 2
1 ♣	1 ♡	No	?		◇ A 9 5 3
					♣ K 9 2

East is worth 2NT. This is the sort of hand where game may be easy with 23 points or so. The recommended point counts for notrump responses are approximate only. An honour in partner's suit increases the chance that the suit is ready to run and so has more than its normal value.

When you play in notrumps, with a suit to run, an ace in another suit will be more valuable than a K Q combination. Minor honours will pull little weight. Thus:

South	West	North	East	♠ A K 10 7 6 2	♠ Q 8
1 ♡	1 ♠	No	1NT	♡ 7 3	♡ A 8 6
No	3 ♠	No	3NT	◇ 9 6 3	◇ A J 5 4
				♣ A 4	♣ J 9 6 3

East–West have an excellent chance of making 3NT. They have nine top tricks unless there is a bad break in the spade suit. If East's ◇ A were the ◇ K Q, the contract would probably fail. Note that East's ♠ Q is an important card, whereas ◇ J and ♣ J may play no part.

Of course, if East's diamond holding were ◇ K Q J x, then 4 ♠ would be a good game. East should realize that with only one heart stop he would have little chance of enjoying any diamond tricks in a notrump contract. At his second turn he would raise to 4 ♠.

Jump Overcalls

The weak jump overcall has its admirers, particularly in
America, but it has two undesirable side effects: you often have
to double on the wrong type of hand; and you must risk bidding
just 1 ♡ over 1 ♣ on a holding such as: ♠ x ♡ A K J x x x
♢ K J x ♣ K x x. Furthermore, we are far from convinced that
pre-emptive jumps achieve anything useful. We prefer to use the
jump overcall on hands of about 13–16 points with a good six-
card suit.

South	West	North	East	West holds: ♠ A Q J 9 6 5
1 ♢	?			♡ A 2
			(love all)	♢ 9 3
				♣ Q 10 6

West's hand is a minimum for an intermediate jump overcall of
2 ♠. Vulnerable, 1 ♠ would suffice.

South	West	North	East	West holds: ♠ A J 3
1 ♡	?			♡ J
			(E–W game)	♢ A K 5
				♣ K 10 9 7 6 2

Here the suit is not good enough for a vulnerable jump
overcall of 3 ♣. West's hand is suitable for play in several
denominations and he should begin with a takeout double. A
jump overcall will normally be based on a suit containing at least
two of the top three honours.

			East holds: ♠ K 6
South	West	North	East
1 ♡	No	1 ♠	?

East holds: ♠ K 6
♡ 8
♢ A K Q 10 7 6 5
♣ Q 10 3

East shows his fine playing strength with a jump overcall of
3 ♢. If West bids 3 ♡ now, this will show a heart stop and deny a
spade stop. In these positions the cue bid is made in the suit
where the stop is held.

Responding to intermediate jump overcalls

Facing an intermediate jump overcall, a raise of the trump suit is constructive and any bid in a new suit is forcing.

				East holds:	♠ K 7
South	*West*	*North*	*East*		♡ 10 9 6 5
1 ♢	2 ♠	No	?		♢ 10 7 3
					♣ A Q J 5

East's most helpful call is 3 ♣. This is not an attempt to compete against his partner's suit; he is just showing where his values lie. West may be able to call 3NT now.

Two-suited Overcalls

As jump overcalls are used to show single suiters of intermediate strength, we are left with two bids to describe two-suiters: 2NT and a cue bid in the opponent's suit.

An immediate overcall of 2NT shows the two lowest unbid suits (the *Unusual Notrump* convention). An overcall in the opponent's suit is presumed initially to be a *Michaels cue bid*, indicating a fair, but more limited, two-suiter. We will look at these two conventions in turn.

The Unusual Notrump

In the second seat a 2NT overcall shows at least five cards in each of the two lowest unbid suits. The bid should be used only when the hand offers a fair chance of eventually buying the contract. Whenever the opponents end up playing the hand, the overcall will greatly assist them in the play. This deal is typical:

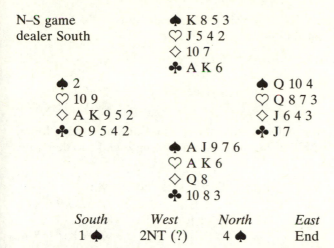

N–S game
dealer South

♠ K 8 5 3
♡ J 5 4 2
♢ 10 7
♣ A K 6

♠ 2
♡ 10 9
♢ A K 9 5 2
♣ Q 9 5 4 2

♠ Q 10 4
♡ Q 8 7 3
♢ J 6 4 3
♣ J 7

♠ A J 9 7 6
♡ A K 6
♢ Q 8
♣ 10 8 3

South	West	North	East
1 ♠	2NT (?)	4 ♠	End

West cashes two rounds of diamonds and switches to ♡ 10. Declarer wins in hand with ♡ A and crosses to ♠ K. Since West's overcall proclaims shortage in the majors, declarer now finesses ♠ J. When this proves to be the right move, he draws the outstanding trump and cashes ♡ K. There is no future in playing for a discard on the heart suit, since West's overcall marks him with 1–2–5–5 distribution. Instead, declarer plays ace, king and another club. West wins and has to give a ruff-and-discard. Without West's overcall, declarer would have little chance of making the contract.

A second danger of launching the unusual notrump on poor hands is that it will warn the opponents of bad breaks and may induce them to stop at a safe level. We therefore recommend that an unusual notrump overcall should be fairly constructive, based on two reasonable suits.

South	West	North	East	West holds: ♠ 10 4
1 ♣	?			♡ 6
		(game all)		♢ A Q J 9 2
				♣ K Q 10 8 6

West bids 2NT, showing the minor suits. His hand is a minimum for the bid when vulnerable.

South	West	North	East	West holds:	♠ J 6
1 ♠	?				♡ 3
		(N–S game)			◇ K J 9 7 2
					♣ A 10 8 6 5

Even at this vulnerability, the hand is quite unsuitable for an overcall of 2NT. It has little playing strength and two defensive high cards.

South	West	North	East	West holds:	♠ 6
1 ◇	?				♡ K Q 9 6 2
		(E–W game)			◇ A
					♣ A K J 6 5 4

West begins with 2NT, showing hearts and clubs. Assuming East chooses one of the suits at the three level, West will give a single raise to show his excellent hand.

It is a common fault for the 2NT caller to bid his hand twice, raising partner's response with little or nothing in reserve. This practice is all too likely to give opponents an easy 500 or so. Remember that when partner names one of your suits at the minimum level he is bidding *your* hand, not his own.

The Michaels cue bid

South	West	North	East
1 ♣	2 ♣		

A minor-suit cue bid shows a two-suiter in the majors, at least 5–4. The usual range is 7–11 (non-vulnerable) or 9–13 (vulnerable), but the sequence may also be adopted on stronger hands. When both majors are held there is more chance to outbid the opponents. Consequently there is less emphasis on holding good suits than with the unusual notrump.

South	West	North	East
1 ♠	2 ♠		

A major-suit cue bid shows a two-suiter in the other major and one of the minors. The suits will be at least 5–5. Here are some examples:

South	West	North	East		
1 ◇	?			West holds:	♠ Q J 8 6 5
			(love all)		♡ K 9 7 4 2
					◇ Q 2
					♣ 6

Not vulnerable, West bids 2◇. Vulnerable, he would have to bite his lip and pass.

South	West	North	East		
1 ◇	?			West holds:	♠ A 10 7 2
			(E–W game)		♡ K Q 9 6 5
					◇ 6
					♣ Q J 6

West's hand is playable in clubs and has the strength required for a takeout double. A double is therefore preferred to a Michaels cue bid.

South	West	North	East		
1 ♠	?			West holds:	♠ J
			(N–S game)		♡ A Q 9 6 2
					◇ 8
					♣ K 10 9 7 6 5

West bids 2 ♠, showing hearts and a minor. Since the bidding will be carried to the three level, fair playing strength is required for this bid. With, say, 4–2–5–2 distribution East must not blithely bid 3 ◇; he must bid 2NT, conventionally asking partner to name his minor suit (which will often be longer than the major).

A Michaels cue bid may also be the launching pad for strong hands:

South	West	North	East		
1 ♣	2 ♣	No	2 ♡	West holds:	♠ K Q 10 8 6 4
No	?		(love all)		♡ A K 9 5 2
					◇ A
					♣ 8

West completes the description of this fine hand with a jump to
3♠.

Michaels cue bids do not apply only in the second seat. After
an opening bid and a response, a cue bid by the player in the
fourth seat has the same general sense:

South	West	North	East
1 ♣	No	1 ◇	2 ♣

East's bid is Michaels, showing a distributional two-suiter in
the majors. A double would also be for takeout but would
suggest a flatter hand with more points.

South	West	North	East
1 ♤	No	2 ◇	2 ♤

Again East's bid is Michaels, showing spades and clubs,
evidently.

In the fourth seat after two passes a cue bid is *not* Michaels. It
shows a powerful hand as in times of yore.

South	West	North	East	East holds:	♠ A Q 10 6 5 2
1 ◇	No	No	?		♤ K 8
		(E–W game)			◇ —
					♣ A Q 10 7 4

The hand is far too strong for 2 ♠ and it is unsatisfactory to
double, as partners have a habit of passing. East should cue-bid
2 ◇, showing a very strong hand. If West bids 2 ♤, East will bid
2 ♠, forcing for one round.

Responding to two-suited overcalls

A jump response in one of the indicated suits shows values but
may be pre-emptive in purpose. A full-blooded game try is
always announced with a further cue bid in the opponent's suit.
In this first example East takes the pre-emptive route:

South	West	North	East	West	East
1 ♦	2 ♦	No	3 ♠	♠ K Q 9 7 2	♠ A J 8 4
				♡ Q 10 8 6 5	♡ J 3
	(N–S game)			♦ 8	♦ Q 7 6 3 2
				♣ J 2	♣ 10 5

West's 2 ♦ is Michaels, showing the majors. East's bid is preemptive, not a game try. He knows the opponents hold the balance of the points and a good fit in clubs, so he makes life difficult for them. On the above hands 3 ♠ is probably only one down and North–South have a likely game in clubs.

When responder has visions of game, he raises his partner's cue bid:

South	West	North	East	West	East
1 ♣	2 ♣	No	3 ♣	♠ A Q 9 6 5	♠ J 10
No	3 ♠	No	4 ♡	♡ K J 6 3	♡ A 10 8 5
				♦ 9 6 3	♦ A Q 10
	(love all)			♣ 4	♣ Q J 7 2

West's 2 ♣ is Michaels and East has enough to invite game. West would rebid 3 ♡ with a minimum. If he wishes to accept the try, as here, he rebids 3 ♠ (longer spades) or 4 ♣ (equal length) or 4 ♡ (longer hearts). These last three responses enable East to choose the better game when he has support for both majors.

Defending against the Unusual Notrump

We must consider how to overcome the inconvenience of a 2NT overcall by the opposition.

South	West	North	East
1 ♡	2NT	?	

When the bidding starts like this, it is foolish not to attach special meaning to the otherwise idle bids of 3 ♣ and 3 ♦. The following scheme is widely played.

North bids: 3 ♣ a sound raise to 3 ♡
             3 ♢ 5 or 6 cards in the other major and three-
                  card support for partner
             3 ♡ a defensive raise to 3 ♡
             dble suggesting that the partnership should play
                  for penalties

Similar responses are used when the opening bid is 1 ♠
(3 ♣—sound raise; 3 ♢—five or six hearts and three-card spade
support; 3 ♠—defensive raise).

South	West	North	East	North holds:	♠ 10 2
1 ♠	2NT	?			♡ A 9 6 4 3
			(love all)		♢ K 10 5 2
					♣ J 9

North should double, showing at least one minor well held and
an interest in penalizing the opponents. Assuming East chooses
one of the minors, South will double with as little as Q 10 x in
trumps.

When North holds a trump fit for opener, it is important not to
be shut out of the auction. The advantage of the defensive raise
can be seen on a hand of this type:

N–S game   ♠ Q J 5 3
dealer South   ♡ K 9 7 2
                       ♢ 9 5 3
                       ♣ 8 4

♠ 9 6   ♠ A 7 4 2
♡ 6   ♡ J 5 3
♢ Q J 10 7 4   ♢ 8 6
♣ K Q 10 9 6   ♣ A J 7 2

                       ♠ K 10 8
                       ♡ A Q 10 8 4
                       ♢ A K 2
                       ♣ 5 3

South opens 1 ♠ and West competes with 2NT. If North passes, intending to show his limited values by a bid of 3 ♠ on the next round, East may jump to 4 ♣ and steal the contract for one down. North should bid 3 ♠ on the way round. This, remember, is a defensive raise, similar to 3 ♠ over a takeout double. With better support North would bid 3 ♣.

SUMMARY

1. Direct raises of an overcall are pre-emptive in nature.
2. A sound raise is indicated by a cue bid in the opener's suit.
3. Opposite an overcall, a bid in a new suit is constructive but non-forcing.
4. Opposite an overcall, a jump shift is forcing for one round.
5. A jump overcall suggests about 12–15 points and a good six-card suit.
6. In the second seat a 2NT overcall shows the two lowest unbid suits (the *Unusual Notrump* convention).
7. In the second seat a bid in the opener's minor suit (such as 1 ♦–2 ♦) is a *Michaels cue bid*, showing a two-suiter in the majors.
8. A major-suit Michaels cue bid (such as 1 ♠–2 ♠) shows a two-suiter in the other major and one of the minors. A response of 2NT asks for the minor.
9. In the fourth seat after two passes a cue bid is not Michaels; it denotes a powerful distributional hand.
10. Facing a two-suited overcall, a jump response in one of the indicated suits may be pre-emptive. A sound game try is indicated by a cue bid in the opener's suit.
11. After 1 ♠–2NT (or 1 ♠–2NT), the third player may bid:
    3 ♣   to show a sound raise to the three level;
    3 ♦   to show three-card support and at least five cards in the other major;
    3 ♠ (or 3 ♠) to show a defensive raise of partner's suit.

7 · Scaling the heights

Slam bidding is a perilous business. Even when you have twelve top tricks to take, the enemy will sometimes surprise you by cashing ♣AK first. On other occasions the side suits will be well under control but the slam will die a slow death because two losers seem to be permanent guests.

The foundation stone of successful slam bidding is not Blackwood, as some players will have you believe: it is the control-showing cue bid.

Cue-bidding

In this context a cue bid is a bid in a new suit when a trump suit has been agreed and there seem to be slam possibilities. Below game level it shows first or second round control in the suit bid and denies a control in any by-passed suit. Say that the bidding begins:

West	East
1 ♡	1 ♠
3 ♠	4 ◇

Spades have been agreed as trumps and East's cue bid of 4 ◇ conveys three important messages:

(a) We are close to a slam;
(b) I control the diamonds;
(c) I do not control the clubs.

If West has no club control either, he will sign off hastily in 4 ♠. Any other advance, such as 4 ♡ or 4NT, would promise a club control.

West may feel he has a problem on this hand:

West	East	West holds: ♠ A Q J 9 2
1 ♠	2 ♡	♡ J 6 2
3 ♡	4 ♣	◇ K Q 3
?		♣ 6 5

With a minimum opening and nothing special in trumps, West may be reluctant to show his diamond control. Nevertheless, he should do so. When partner is making the running in a slam venture you should generally co-operate by showing your controls. So long as this doesn't carry you beyond game, you promise no extra strength.

A cue bid above game level normally shows a first-round control. You can often indicate a second-round control by a cue bid in another suit:

West	East	East holds: ♠ K 10 9 5
1 ♠	3 ♠	♡ Q 9 8 2
4 ◇	?	◇ A J 7 3
		♣ 6

A cue bid of 5 ♣ now would suggest first-round control of clubs. Instead, East should cue-bid 5 ◇, which will logically promise second-round club control and will deny a control in hearts.

Cue-bidding shortages

A cue bid is usually based on an ace or king, but there are occasions when a singleton (or void) may prove critical. A singleton will not necessarily contribute to the playing strength (unless in the short trump hand), but as a control it is just as effective as a king—safer, in fact.

West	East	East holds: ♠ A 10 9 3
1 ♠	3 ♠	♡ Q 9 4
4 ♣	?	◇ 7
		♣ K 8 7 4 2

East bids 4 $\diamondsuit$. If his partner bids 4 $\heartsuit$ now, there are excellent chances that the hands fit well. East will show the suitability of his hand by going past game with a cue bid of 5 $\clubsuit$. This will not promise first-round control because partner has already cue-bid the suit.

It is a sound rule never to cue-bid a shortage in a suit bid by partner. If you do and he is looking at A Q J x x (or K Q J x x), he will assume you have the missing honour.

The advance cue bid

Usually a suit is explicitly agreed before a cue bid is made, but sometimes the cue bid itself fixes the trump suit:

	(1)				(2)	
	1 $\spadesuit$	2NT			1 $\diamondsuit$	2 $\heartsuit$
	3 $\heartsuit$	4 $\clubsuit$			2 $\spadesuit$	3 $\heartsuit$
					4 $\clubsuit$	

In both cases 4 $\clubsuit$ could hardly be natural. It is an advance cue bid agreeing hearts as trumps.

Responding on strong hands

A jump shift promises either a strong single-suited hand or big trump support for the opener. Strong balanced hands and two-suiters must follow a different route, as we will see.

Two-suiters

With a two-suiter you need time. You don't jump on the first round, because the sequence will be forcing when you show your second suit.

West	East		East holds:	$\spadesuit$ 6
1 $\spadesuit$	2 $\diamondsuit$			$\heartsuit$ A 9
2 $\spadesuit$	3 $\clubsuit$			$\diamondsuit$ A K J 6 5
3NT	4 $\clubsuit$			$\clubsuit$ A Q 9 7 2

East has shown an excellent hand by pressing on so strongly on an apparent misfit. If West signs off in 4NT now, East will give up.

Strong balanced hands

All balanced hands of 16 points or more qualify for the *Baron 2NT response*.

The Acol response of 2NT on 11 to 12 points is well liked by many rubber bridge players, and we recognize that it often produces good results. However, tournament players need to be accurate in slam bidding, so we incline to the alternative Baron 2NT. (Flat hands of 16 to 19 points, by the way, are often a problem in traditional systems.) These examples show the Baron 2NT (16 or more) at work:

West	*East*	East holds:	♠ K 6
1 ♡	2NT		♡ A Q 10 5
3 ♢	?		♢ Q J 5
			♣ A J 9 2

East should bid 4 ♡ to show good trump support and a limited 2NT bid. This is a clearer call than 3 ♡, which might be made on ♡ Q x x.

West	*East*	East holds:	♠ A 7
1 ♠	2NT		♡ K Q 10 2
3 ♡	?		♢ Q 6 3
			♣ A K 6 5

East bids 4 ♣, an advance cue bid. This (for the moment, at any rate) agrees hearts as trumps, since with spade support he could have bid 3 ♠.

West	*East*	East holds:	♠ Q 6
1 ♠	2NT		♡ A K 10 4
3 ♢	?		♢ K J 2
			♣ A Q J 6

No fit has emerged, but East is too good to sign off in 3NT. He bids 3 ♡ and awaits further developments. If West bids an uninspiring 3NT, East will show his values with a limit raise to 4NT.

With a hand that would previously have qualified for a limit 2NT response, you must adopt a suit-over-suit style (usually two of a minor) and bid 2NT on the next round.

Single-suiters

Having stated that two-suiters and strong balanced hands do *not* qualify for a jump shift, we are left with two types of hand on which a jump shift should be used: single-suiters and hands with excellent trump support.

West	East	East holds:	♠ A J 5
1 ♡	3 ♣		♡ 6
3 ♡	?		◇ A 10 8
			♣ A K J 6 3 2

Having passed a strong hint of slam chances, the responder eases back on the second round by bidding 3NT.

Hands with strong trump support

West	East	East holds:	♠ K 6
1 ♡	3 ♣		♡ A Q 9 3
3 ◇	?		◇ J 4
			♣ A Q 10 5 4

East rebids 4 ♡, showing primary trump support but little to spare for his jump shift. If he were *stronger*, East would bid only 3 ♡ for the moment.

West	East	East holds:	♠ K J 9 3
1 ♠	3 ◇		♡ Q 6
3 ♠	?		◇ A K 10 8 5
			♣ A 4

Here East bids 4 ♣—an advance cue bid agreeing spades as trumps. 4 ♣ is not an ambiguous call since East would not embark on a jump shift with a minor two-suiter.

4NT has many meanings

Some people play that 4NT is 'always Blackwood, partner'. There won't be any silly misunderstandings, we will concede that. But these players lose accuracy in the slam zone. There are several different meanings of 4NT and it is important to pin them down.

When 4NT is a limit bid

4NT is a limit bid whenever it is a raise of a natural notrump bid. These 4NT bids are all non-forcing:

(1)	1NT	4NT	(2)	1 ◇	2 ♣	(3)	1 ♠	2 ♣
				3NT	4NT		2 ♡	3NT
							4NT	

The only apparent exception to this rule is when the responder has made a jump shift:

(4)	1 ♠	3 ♡
	3NT	4NT

Here 4NT is Blackwood; otherwise responder would have no way to turn on hands such as ♠ K x ♡ A K Q J x x x ◇ x ♣ A K x.

When 4NT is a sign-off

In an ideal world all slams could be investigated below the 3NT level. This is often not possible, of course, but the partnership should be able to come to rest in 4NT. *A player who has previously bid notrumps may spurn his partner's four-level slam advance by signing off in 4NT.* We are thinking of auctions of this type:

West	East	West holds: ♠ K Q 7 5 4
1 ♠	2 ♣	♡ A Q J
3NT	4 ♣	◇ K Q 3
4NT		♣ 8 5

West is not inspired by thoughts of a club slam. He signs off in 4NT and metaphorically folds his fan.

West	East	East holds:	♠ 9 3
1 ♠	2 ♣		♡ Q 10 2
2 ♡	3NT		◇ A Q 9 3
4 ♣	4NT		♣ K Q 6 5

This time responder dampens his partner's ambitions with a call of 4NT.

When 4NT is Blackwood

4NT is Blackwood when a suit has been clearly agreed, as in these examples:

(1)	1 ♠	2 ♡	(2)	1 ◇	1 ♠	(3)	1 ♡	4NT
	4 ♡	4NT		2 ♣	2 ♡			
				3 ♠	4NT			

In sequence (3) responder is presumably agreeing hearts, but he may instead hold a solid suit of his own.

Sometimes trump agreement is implicit because there is no room to support the suit:

(1)	1 ♡	2 ♣	(2)	1 ♠	2NT
	2 ♠	4 ♣		4 ♠	4NT
	4NT				

4NT is Blackwood in both these cases. (Remember that East's 2NT in the second example is unlimited.)

The standard set of Blackwood responses is wasteful of space. A variant of the scheme known, rather quaintly, as five-ace Blackwood conveys more information. This is the system of responses:

5 ♣	0 or 3 aces
5 ◇	1 or 4 aces
5 ♡	2 aces
5 ♠	2 aces and one key king
5NT	2 aces and two key kings

A 'key king' is one in a critical suit, such as trumps or a main side suit.

When 4NT is a general slam try

A player who has embarked on a constructive auction may bid a natural 4NT *en route*. When no suit has been clearly agreed, 4NT will indicate values to spare and continued interest in a slam.

West	East	
1 ♡	2 ♠	West holds: ♠ 6
3 ♣	3 ♡	♡ K Q 10 5
3NT	4 ♢	♢ K Q 8 7
?		♣ K Q 9 6

With 15 points which may all be working, West is too good to close shop in four hearts. Instead he bids 4NT, non-conventional but forward-going.

West	East	
1 ♠	2 ♡	East holds: ♠ K 4
3 ♣	3 ♢	♡ A Q 9 6 5
3 ♡	3 ♠	♢ A 10 7 2
4 ♣	?	♣ J 3

From East's point of view it is not clear what, if any, is the agreed suit. He bids 4NT, a general slam try.

5NT—a new look at the grand slam force

5NT is a trump asking bid, even when it follows a Blackwood 4NT. In the original (Josephine) version partner was required to bid the grand if he had two of the three top honours, to bid the small slam if he had none, and to call 6 ♣ with one. This is all right when the auction has begun, say, 1 ♡–3 ♡; but the quality of support will often be much less. Take this auction, for example:

West	East
1 ♠	2 ♣
3 ♠	3NT
4 ◇	4 ♠
5NT	?

East may hold as little as a low singleton trump on this auction, so the standard scheme will be no use to West if he holds, say, ♠ A K Q x x x or ♠ A K J x x x x. We propose a far more sensible approach to the 5NT bid: *the responder to a 5NT grand slam force should consider whether, in relation to his bidding so far, his trump holding is* (a) *minimum,* (b) *about as expected,* (c) *somewhat better than partner may expect.*

Because the possibilities are so numerous, it is impractical to draw up an exact schedule of responses; for one thing, there is much less room when the slam is intended in a minor suit. On the auction considered above, the responder might allocate the responses like this:

6 ♣	low singleton
6 ◇	J or x x
6 ♡	Q, J x or x x x
6 ♠	Q x, K or A
6NT	Q J or better

When the trump suit is clubs, the responder must judge whether his holding is good enough to by-pass the small slam:

West	East
1 ♠	3 ♣
4 ♣	4 ♡
5 ◇	5NT
?	

East's jump shift proclaims a strong club suit, so he can hardly be missing two honours when he bids 5NT. West may respond above the 6 ♣ level when he holds one of the top honours.

The 5NT bid can be used also by the lesser trump hand:

West	East	West holds: ♠ A 3
1 ♡	3 ◇	♡ A K 9 6 2
4 ◇	5 ♣	◇ J 9 3 2
5NT		♣ K J

East, whose suit is again known to be a good one, would reply on this schedule:

6 ♣   A 10 x x x x, K 10 x x x x

6 ◇   K Q x x x, A Q x x x, A K x x x

6 ♡   A K Q x x, A K x x x x

SUMMARY

1. A cue bid shows:
   (a) interest in a slam;
   (b) first or (below game level) second round control in the bid suit;
   (c) no control in any by-passed suit.
2. The *Baron 2NT response* is made on balanced hands of 16 points or more.
3. A jump shift promises a powerful single-suiter or a hand with good trump support. A pronounced two-suiter does not qualify for a jump shift.
4. A bid of 4NT is:
   (a) natural, when it is a raise of a notrump bid;
   (b) a sign-off, when a player who has previously bid notrumps spurns his partner's four-level slam advance;
   (c) 5-ace Blackwood when a trump suit has been clearly agreed;
   (d) in other circumstances, a general slam try.
5. The responder to a 5NT grand slam force indicates whether, in relation to his bidding so far, his trump holding is (a) minimum, (b) about as expected, (c) better than expected.

8 · Protection

When the opponents' auction peters out at a low level and you are sitting in the pass-out seat, do you say to yourself 'They won't do us much harm here' and pass? Wrong! Even if your own hand is not too sparkling, the opponents' lack of ambition suggests that your partner has fair values. You can probably find a playable spot somewhere or push the opponents one level higher.

There are two main cases where protection has to be considered and we will look at them in turn.

The opening bid runs to the fourth player

What is East to think in this situation:

South	West	North	East		East holds:	♠ K 10 8 2
1 ♡	No	No	?			♡ 6 4
						◇ A 9 7 3
						♣ K 8 5

South opened with a one-bid and North was too weak to reply. It is quite likely that East–West have the balance of the cards. Certainly East should contest the part score with a takeout double.

Partnerships with no understanding of the principles of protection suffer one of two fates. Either they give the opponents right of way on more than their fair share of part scores; or they have to take risks in the second seat, often with predictable consequences.

A suit overcall in the fourth seat may be based on quite modest values:

South	West	North	East	East holds:	♠ A 2
1 ♡	No	No	?		♡ 9 4
					◇ K 9 8 5 4 2
					♣ J 10 7

East's hand does not amount to much, but he should compete with 2 ◇ nevertheless.

Since a suit overcall in the protective seat may be light, the requirements for the jump overcall are reduced:

South	West	North	East	East holds:	♠ A Q J 8 7 2
1 ◇	No	No	?		♡ A 4
					◇ 7
					♣ J 9 6 5

At any vulnerability East is worth 2 ♠.

A call of 1NT in the protective position shows around 11–14 points. It is likely to be upper range over 1 ♣ or 1 ◇, though, since partner had every chance to speak with reasonable values.

Two-way 2 ♣ bid in the fourth position

Since to double and then bid notrumps would herald 18 points or so, an awkward gap arises for hands in the 15–17 range. This can be neatly filled by playing a two-way 2 ♣ bid—either natural or balanced in the middle range. This is the scheme:

South	West	North	East
1 ♠	No	No	2 ♣
No	?		

West bids: 2 ◇ or 2 ♡   a sign-off on the assumption that East has the balanced hand.

2 ♠   shows at least 9 points and requests East to clarify his hand. East will rebid 2NT with the 15–17 type.

2NT   natural, assuming a club suit opposite.

It follows that when the fourth player has only a moderate club suit he must reopen with 1NT, not 2 ♣.

A call of 2NT in the protective seat is tactical, based on a strong minor suit. Over 1 ♡, a hand such as ♠ J 6 ♡ K 10 5 ◇ A K Q 9 6 4 ♣ K 8 would qualify for 2NT.

When not to protect in the fourth seat

When the opening bid was 1 ♣ or 1 ◇, there is less reason to suppose the second player has fair values than over a major suit opening. East must pause to consider in this situation:

South	West	North	East
1 ♣	No	No	?

East holds: ♠ 6 4
♡ K J 7 5 2
◇ K 9 8
♣ K 5 3

East's playing strength justifies competing with 1 ♡, but the wise course is to pass. West was unable to overcall at the one level and it is quite likely that the opponents have a spade fit. With East's majors reversed it would not be unreasonable to compete with 1 ♠.

The same considerations apply when the player in the protective seat has a balanced hand:

South	West	North	East
1 ♣	No	No	?

East holds: ♠ K 8 3
♡ K 9 5
◇ 10 7 4
♣ A Q 8 3

Again East should pass. West would surely have found something to say over 1 ♣ with twelve points or more, so it is most unlikely that East–West can make a game.

Protecting when the opponents have found a trump fit

When the opponents have found a trump fit, it is good odds that your side has one, too. If they find a trump fit and yet stop at a low level, it is a fair bet also that the points are equally divided. In short, the conditions are at their most favourable for protection.

South	West	North	East	West holds: ♠ K 10 8 2
1 ♡	No	2 ♡	No	♡ 6 5
No	?			◇ J 9 6
				♣ A 10 7 5

West should keep the bidding alive with a double. His partner is marked with 10 points or so. Indeed it is rarely right to sell out to a two-level trump fit. On the present hand East has no need to proffer his neck on some balanced 12- or 13- count. He knows his partner will be very ready to protect if South passes.

This auction offers fair prospects also:

South	West	North	East	East holds: ♠ K 10 8 2
1 ♣	No	1NT	No	♡ K J 7 5 4
2 ♣	No	No	?	◇ Q 10 3
				♣ 6

East should venture a takeout double. North surely holds at least three clubs, so the opponents have found a trump fit.

As we have noted, when the opponents have stopped low in a trump fit there is good reason for protecting. When they have not found a fit these arguments apply in reverse. Firstly, a misfit for one side is frequently a misfit for the other. Secondly, there is less reason to suppose the points are equally divided. The enemy may have sensed the misfit and stopped low on quite a respectable point count. Perhaps the most important reason, though, is that the opponents will be quick to pull the trigger. Two misfitting hands can prove devastating in defence. Discretion is therefore advisable after this type of auction:

South	West	North	East	East holds: ♠ 8 4
1 ♡	No	1 ♠	No	♡ Q 2
2 ♡	No	No	?	◇ K Q 9 6 5
				♣ K 10 7 2

Many players would double now or bid an 'unusual' 2NT. This action is quite unsound. North may well hold up to 10 points and as he has no liking for hearts he may have the minors well held.

Protecting at rubber bridge

At rubber bridge the principles of protection still apply. There are, however, two factors that make protection less attractive than in the duplicate game. Firstly, the opponents' bidding may be less reliable. There is always the danger that they have underbid their hands and will be grateful for a second bite at the cherry. Secondly, if you push them up from 1 ♡ to 1NT or some two-level contract, this represents a very small gain for your side. In pairs play you would be obliged to contest further, dicing with death, but at rubber bridge you would not take such a risk.

SUMMARY

1. When an opening bid in a major suit runs to the fourth player, he should reopen freely.
2. In the protective position 1NT suggests 11–14 points. It will be upper range against a minor-suit opening.
3. In the protective position, 2 ♣ is two-way. It shows either a club suit or a 15–17 balanced hand. In response, partner may sign off in two of a new suit, cue-bid with 9 points or more, or bid a natural 2NT.
4. In the protective position 2NT is a tactical call, based on a long minor suit.
5. When the opponents have found a trump fit but have stopped at a low level, conditions are at their most favourable for protection.
6. When the opponents have not found a trump fit, be more cautious about protecting.

9 · The 1NT battleground

The weak notrump opening is the first salvo of many tactical battles, especially in the pairs game. The mathematics of the part score ensure that the declarer in 1NT rarely scores a bad board when non-vulnerable. If he loses 100 by going two down, the opponents will usually find they had an easy 110 or 140 available somewhere. In the modern style defenders are willing to take considerable risks to dislodge the 1NT bidder. The most effective defences to 1NT are those that allow entry to the auction as often as possible. We advocate the Cansino defence, which was designed with just that purpose in mind.

The Cansino defence to 1NT

This defence uses two conventional overcalls, 2 ♣ and 2 ◇. They apply in both the second and fourth seats.

    2 ♣   shows a hand playable in clubs and two other suits; usual strength, about 10–14.

    2 ◇   shows a hand playable in three suits, barring clubs.

Responding to 2 ♣

The responder may pass 2 ♣ or seek a fit elsewhere by bidding his lowest suit. This is a neat example:

South	West	North	East	West	East
1NT	2 ♣	No	2 ◇	♠ A 10 8 2	♠ K 9 6 3
No	2 ♡	No	2 ♠	♡ K J 10 7 4	♡ 8 2
				◇ 4	◇ A 10 7 2
				♣ K Q 3	♣ 8 5 4

East knows that West must be playable in diamonds or spades,

so he bids 2 $\diamondsuit$ in preference to passing 2 $\clubsuit$. The spade fit comes
to light when West denies diamonds.

With a good hand, offering game prospects, responder may
begin with a conventional 2NT. The overcaller rebids 3 $\clubsuit$ with a
singleton heart, 3 $\diamondsuit$ with a singleton spade, and 3NT with a
singleton diamond.

South	West	North	East	West	East
1NT	2 $\clubsuit$	No	2NT	$\spadesuit$ K Q 9 2	$\spadesuit$ J 8 5 4
No	3 $\clubsuit$	No	4 $\spadesuit$	$\heartsuit$ 8	$\heartsuit$ A K Q 3 2
				$\diamondsuit$ A J 8 5 4	$\diamondsuit$ 9 2
				$\clubsuit$ Q 6 3	$\clubsuit$ K 8

East, assured of a fit in one major, bids a conventional 2NT.
When partner announces a singleton heart, he jumps to the
spade game.

A jump bid in response to 2 $\clubsuit$ must logically show a suit
playable opposite a (likely) singleton. It will be something like
K J 10 9 x x with perhaps an ace and a king outside.

Responding to 2 $\diamondsuit$

The 2 $\diamondsuit$ overcall shows a hand playable in diamonds, hearts or
spades.

				East holds: $\spadesuit$ J 10 5 4
South	West	North	East	$\heartsuit$ 9 3
1NT	2 $\diamondsuit$	No	?	$\diamondsuit$ Q 9 6 2
				$\clubsuit$ A J 5

East should prefer 2 $\spadesuit$ to a pass. He might as well play in a
major and his own hand (about which less is known) will become
the declarer.

Responder's only forcing bid is 3 $\diamondsuit$.

South	West	North	East	West	East
1NT	2 $\diamondsuit$	No	3 $\diamondsuit$	$\spadesuit$ A 10 9 5 2	$\spadesuit$ K 8 3
No	3 $\spadesuit$	No	4 $\spadesuit$	$\heartsuit$ K J 5	$\heartsuit$ Q 9 2
				$\diamondsuit$ A 8 4 2	$\diamondsuit$ K J 10 3
				$\clubsuit$ 9	$\clubsuit$ A 10 7

East forces with 3 $\diamond$ and raises to game when his partner shows what must be at least a four-card suit of spades.

Doubling Situations

When 1NT is doubled, the third player must be allowed to seek sanctuary in any of the four suits. The Stayman convention and transfer bids are no longer used. If 1NT doubled seems a dismal spot, it is worth attempting a rescue even when the odds of improving the contract are not too bright. Shapely hands offer an easier escape than flat hands. This is a popular manoeuvre:

South	West	North	East	North holds:	♠ Q 10 5 2
1NT	dble	2 ♣!	dble		♡ 8 7 6 3
No	No	redble			◇ J 7 5 4
					♣ 6

North's SOS redouble asks his partner to choose one of the other three suits. Most players would risk this sequence even when vulnerable; it is extremely rare for both opponents to pass two clubs.

When the third player does bid over the double, this can cause a problem for the second defender:

				East holds:	♠ K 10 8 4
South	West	North	East		♡ 6 5 2
1NT	dble	2 ◇	?		◇ 7 2
					♣ A 9 6 3

East has no wish to sell out to 2 ◇, but what can he do? A bid of 2 ♠ might hit partner's doubleton or cross his intention to punish 2 ◇. The solution is for East–West to agree that they will never give best to two of a minor in this situation. East can then make a *forcing pass* on the present hand, giving his partner the chance to double (for penalties) or contest in some other way.

Double by the fourth player

It is common practice for the partner of the 1NT opener to make some show of strength when he is weak and fears a double. He may extend his feathers with a Stayman call or perhaps a transfer bid. To counter this, all doubles by the fourth player show a strong hand. They suggest that he would have doubled 1NT.

South	West	North	East	East holds:	♠ A 10 5
1NT	No	2 ◇¹	?		♡ K J 3
					◇ Q 7 4
¹Transfer to 2 ♡					♣ A K 9 2

East doubles to show a flattish hand of 15 points or more. Sometimes East can turn the transfer to his own advantage:

South	West	North	East	East holds:	♠ K J 8 4
1NT	No	2 ◇¹	?		♡ 5
					◇ A Q 9 6
¹Transfer to 2 ♡					♣ Q 10 8 5

Now East bids 2 ♡ (the enemy suit) for takeout.

When the fourth hand aspires to punish the eventual contract, he must pass initially:

South	West	North	East	East holds:	♠ A 5 3
1NT	No	2 ◇¹	No		♡ A J 10 8
2 ♡	No	No	dble		◇ K Q 7 2
¹Transfer to 2 ♡					♣ A 9

East's second-round double is for penalties. Had he doubled on the first round as well, the second double would be penalty-oriented but would show less in the trump suit.

When the third player makes a natural weak takeout, a double again shows points. It looks towards penalties, but does not guarantee more than three cards in the opponent's suit:

South	West	North	East	West holds:	♠ A 9 6 2
1NT	No	2 ♡	dble		♡ 9 5 4
No	?				◇ K 7 5 4
					♣ 10 3

Here West would let the double stand, expecting his two high cards to aid the defence. There is no reason to suppose that 2 ♠ would produce a better result. Of course, North will occasionally turn up with a fair suit and find ♣ A Q J in the dummy. That is no reason to let the opponents escape on the majority of hands.

Double by a passed hand

A double by a player who has passed shows a two-suiter, either in the majors or the minors. The responder will usually bid his longer minor:

South	West	North	East	East holds:	♠ K 10 3
No	No	1NT	No		♡ J 4
No	dble	No	?		◇ A 10 8 5 2
					♣ J 9 7

East bids 2 ◇. If his partner shows the majors by bidding 2 ♡, East will give preference to 2 ♠. The same scheme applies to *all* doubles of a strong notrump, because then it is never advisable to double for penalties.

The 2NT overcall

It is futile to double when you have a powerful two-suiter offering a fair chance of game. An overcall of 2NT alerts partner to the good news and requests a transfer to 3 ♣. Then you bid your *higher* suit, intending to show the second suit on the next round. This example shows the idea:

South	West	North	East	West holds:	♠ K Q 8 7 5 2
1NT	2NT	No	3 ♣		♡ J
No	3 ♠	No	3NT		◇ A K J 9 6 4
No	4 ◇	No	?		♣ —

A 2NT overcall by a passed hand will be the Unusual Notrump convention, showing the minor suits. It is also best to assume this treatment when the third player has made a weakness takeout in a major suit. All these 2NT bids show the minors:

	South	West	North	East
(a)	1NT	No	2 ♡	No
	No	2NT		
(b)	1NT	No	2 ♡¹	No
	2 ♠	2NT		
		¹*Transfer to 2 ♠*		
(c)	1NT	No	2 ♠	2NT
(d)	1NT	No	2 ♣	No
	2 ♡	No	No	2NT

The Lebensohl Convention

A major-suit overcall, especially 2 ♠, often causes problems for the player in the third seat. Standard practice is hardly satisfactory and it is worth mastering Lebensohl, the best convention in this area. We are considering this type of situation:

North holds: ♠ 7 4
♡ K J 9 7 6 5
◇ J 8
♣ K J 4

South	West	North	East
1NT	2 ♠	?	

North wants to compete with 3 ♡, but will partner read it as forcing? Or perhaps North has a 13-count with five hearts. Now he wants 3 ♡ to be forcing, but perhaps partner will pass...

The Lebensohl convention attacks this problem. All bids at the three level are forcing. 2NT is a transfer to 3 ♣, after which the responder may pass or sign off in another suit. These are examples of the convention at work:

North holds: ♠ 9 6
♡ K Q 7 4
◇ Q 3
♣ A Q 10 6 2

South	West	North	East
1NT	2 ♠	?	

North bids 3 ♣ (forcing). If there is a heart fit, it will soon come to light.

South	West	North	East	North holds: ♠ 9 5 2
1NT	2 ♡	2NT	No	♡ 6
3 ♣	No	3 ◇		◇ Q J 8 5 4 2
				♣ A J 7

North's sequence is not invitational. His partner must pass.

South	West	North	East	North holds: ♠ K J 9 6 5 2
1NT	2 ♡	2NT	No	♡ J 4
3 ♣	No	3 ♠		◇ A 10 9 4
				♣ 3

Here North could have signed off in 2 ♠. His bid of 3 ♠ via Lebensohl is therefore invitational. A direct jump to 3 ♠ would have been forcing.

What meanings should we give to these four sequences (and their equivalent when the overcall is in hearts)?

	South	West	North	East
(a)	1NT	2 ♠	3NT	
(b)	1NT	2 ♠	2NT	No
	3 ♣	No	3NT	
(c)	1NT	2 ♠	3 ♠	
(d)	1NT	2 ♠	2NT	No
	3 ♣	No	3 ♠	

The first sequence is to play, and North shows a spade guard. The second sequence also indicates a desire to play in 3NT, but it denies a spade stop. When the opener is also bare in the suit of the overcall, the partnership may settle in four of a minor.

Sequences (c) and (d) are Staymanic. They guarantee four cards in the other major, hearts in this instance. Once again the direct sequence (c) shows a stop in the enemy suit. The sequence via Lebensohl (d) denies one.

What to do with an 11-count

Playing Lebensohl involves the loss of the natural 2NT

response—a worth-while exchange in our view. A bid must be found in this situation, though:

				North holds:	♠ 9 5 2
South	*West*	*North*	*East*		♡ A Q 8
1NT	2 ♠	?			◇ K 10 9 5
					♣ Q 9 3

North doubles, suggesting around 11 points and a balanced hand. No holding in the opponent's suit is promised and the opener may remove the double on an unsuitable hand. With a hand such as ♠ Q 10 8 5 ♡ A 4 2 ◇ J 10 5 ♣ 10 7 3 North would have to pass 2 ♠ and take an undoubled penalty.

SUMMARY

1. *Cansino defence to 1NT*: 2 ♣ shows a hand playable in clubs and two other suits; 2 ◇ shows a hand playable in three suits, barring clubs.
2. After 1NT–dble–2 ♣ or 2 ◇, a pass by the fourth player is forcing.
3. When the responder to 1NT bids at the two level, a double by the fourth player is similar to a double of 1NT.
4. Doubles of 1NT by a passed hand show a two-suiter, either in the majors or the minors. The same is true of all doubles of a strong notrump.
5. After a 1NT opening a 2NT overcall shows a powerful two-suiter. The responder bids 3 ♣, after which the overcaller shows his higher suit.

The Lebensohl convention

6. When 1NT has been overcalled with two of a major, 2NT by the third player is a transfer to 3 ♣; all three-level bids are forcing.
7. A three-level bid via the Lebensohl 2NT transfer is a sign-off,

except that if the suit could have been called at the two level, it is now a game try.

8. 3NT, bid directly, shows a stop in the enemy suit. 3NT via the Lebensohl transfer denies one.

9. A cue bid is Staymanic. If bid directly, it shows a stop in the enemy suit. A cue bid via Lebensohl denies a stop.

10 · Defending against strong club systems

From time to time you will encounter players who have adopted one club systems, usually Precision or Blue Club. You will have to consider the best form of defence.

Many pundits will tell you that the weakness of the 1 ♣ systems lies in their vulnerability to interference before genuine suits have been named. This may seem a reasonable idea, but things don't always work out that way at the table. The stronger side, if it gains the final contract, often benefits from the information it has been given. Furthermore, it is wrong to suppose that low-level intervention will throw the 1 ♣ bidders out of their stride. Partners who play such systems will have a method to express immediately the nature and strength of their hands.

So, we do not support those who think it is clever to overcall with ♠ K 10 x x x and a queen. Overcalls should be based on a good suit. This is the scheme when the opponents have opened with a strong club:

Suit bids	natural
Double	spades and diamonds
1NT	hearts and clubs
2NT	the minors

If you want a mnemonic to distinguish between double and 1NT, think of 'Double Diamond'.

Raises of an indicated suit are pre-emptive and bids in a new suit are natural. In the following examples the 1 ♣ opening is always strong.

South	West	North	East	West holds: ♠ 7 5
1 ♣	?			♡ K Q 10 9 6 4 2
		(love all)		◇ 3
				♣ Q 10 8

This being no time for caution, West bids 3 ♡. Vulnerable, he would bid 2 ♡ only.

South	West	North	East	East holds: ♠ K 10 3
				♡ J 4
1 ♣	1 ♠	No	?	◇ Q 9 6 5 4 2
				♣ 8 4

East has enough to raise to 2 ♠. This mild effort at preemption may well inconvenience the 1 ♣ opener. A bid from him now such as 3 ♣ will have to cover a wide range. Even if he has the shape for a takeout double, his partner will have little room to express his type.

Overcalling on two-suiters

When you hold two suits there is more chance that partner can assist you:

South	West	North	East	West holds: ♠ 7
1 ♣	?			♡ K Q 8 7 2
		(N–S game)		◇ 5
				♣ K J 10 8 6 3

West bids 1NT, showing hearts and clubs. On this hand West has some chance of fighting the opposition. To bid 1NT on a nondescript collection such as ♠ 8 ♡ Q J 10 7 2 ◇ 6 4 ♣ Q J 9 8 5 is worse than pointless. Prospects of winning the contract are negligible and the opponents will often capitalize on the information gained.

When the overcaller is strong

With a strong balanced hand (obviously rare) the best course is to pass initially:

South	West	North	East	West holds:	♠ 7 5
1 ♣	?				♡ A K 10 4
		(game all)			◇ K J 9 3
					♣ A 9 8

West passes on the first round. If the opponents bid 1 ♣–1 ◇–
1 ♠, West can compete with a takeout double on the second
round. Otherwise he should not contest. Note that the
conventional meaning of a double (showing spades and
diamonds) applies only on the round of bidding that starts with
1 ♣.

With a powerful two-suiter start with a natural bid at the
lowest level:

South	West	North	East	West holds:	♠ K Q 10 8 5
1 ♣	?				♡ 7 3
		(game all)			◇ —
					♣ A Q J 9 7 2

West bids simply 2 ♣. Later he will complete the picture by
rebidding strongly in spades.

Defending in the fourth seat

The fourth hand may employ the same tactics of 1NT and
double:

South	West	North	East	East holds:	♠ Q J 10 7 2
1 ♣	No	1 ♡	?		♡ 6
		(N–S game)			◇ K Q 9 8 2
					♣ J 7

Whether North's response is natural (Precision) or artificial
(Blue Club), East can double to show spades and diamonds.

A *natural* suit response may change the conventional
meanings of 1NT and double by the fourth player:

After 1 ♣–No–1 ♡   1NT shows spades and clubs
After 1 ♣–No–1 ♠   double shows hearts and diamonds

So, the suit bid naturally by responder is replaced by the other suit of the same rank.

After a natural response at the two level, 2NT by fourth hand shows the two lowest unbid suits and double again shows spades and diamonds (except after 1 ♣–No–2 ◇, when it shows spades and clubs).

Defending against a strong 2 ♣ opening

The side that opens 2 ♣ can presumably make a game somewhere. It is still a moot point whether, by intervening on moderate hands, you will assist opponents to make their eventual contract or will enable your side to sacrifice effectively.

For example, the bidding begins:

				East holds:	♠ K Q 9 8 4
South	*West*	*North*	*East*		♡ 3
2 ♣	No	2 ♡	?		◇ Q 10 7 6 5 3
					♣ J

At favourable vulnerability, in a pairs, it may be right for East to double, indicating defensive possibilities in diamonds and spades; but there is a substantial danger, even then, that the effect of the intervention will be to warn the opponents of the proverbial 'rocks of distribution'.

SUMMARY

1. Undisciplined intervention against a strong club opening often helps the opponents when they win the contract. Overcall only when holding a good suit.
2. After a strong 1 ♣ opening this scheme applies:

Suit bids	are natural
Double	shows spades and diamonds
1NT	shows hearts and clubs
2NT	shows the minors

3. After an artificial response to 1 ♣, the defensive scheme in the fourth seat is the same as in the second seat.
4. After a natural response to 1 ♣, the suits shown by double, 1NT and 2NT may change. 2NT always shows the two lowest unbid suits; double and 1NT show a combination in which the suit bid by responder may be replaced by the other suit of equal rank.
5. The same methods are employed against a strong 2 ♣ opening.

11 · The multi-coloured 2 ◇

'This convention, first expounded in depth by Terence Reese, has been widely adopted by tournament players because it combines two important objectives; economy in the use of bids and confusion of the opponents.' Such is the slightly awesome introduction to the Multi in *The Bridge Player's Alphabetical Handbook*, by Reese and Dormer.

The Multi is fairly young in the scale of time, and the account that follows is slightly different from that of the *Handbook*, which fitted best with a 1 ♣ system. The rather complicated way of expressing strong three-suiters has been abandoned. In the present scheme an opening bid of 2 ◇ shows:

(1) a weak two bid in hearts or spades, or
(2) an Acol two bid in clubs or diamonds, or
(3) a balanced hand of 20–22 points.

In addition to the admirable economy of such a bid, it has proved an extremely difficult opening for opponents to counter. Many are the sad tales of players at international level ending in absurd contracts after a 2 ◇ opening by the opponents. Of course the opener's partner must be able to decipher the bid himself. The general approach is that he assumes it to be a 'weak two' type until informed otherwise.

When used as a weak two bid, the 2 ◇ opening should be viewed as part of a unified system, not as a baton to be vaguely brandished. The great Italian partnerships set the example here; they *always* play their systems accurately.

The 2 ♡ response

This is the most frequent response. It indicates that two hearts is the limit of the hand if the opener has a weak two in hearts. The opener's rebid clarifies his hand type as follows:

Pass   weak two in hearts, normally 7–10 with a six-card suit
2 ♠   weak two in spades
2NT   20–22 balanced
3 ♣   Acol two in clubs
3 ♢   Acol two in diamonds

The last two rebids show a powerful hand but are not forcing, since the Acol 2 ♣ opening is available for hands of game-force strength. Admittedly, it is not ideal to begin to describe your hand at this level, but such hands are rare.

These are typical sequences:

West	East	West	East
2 ♢	2 ♡	♠ A Q 10 7 6 2	♠ K 9 8 3
2 ♠	3 ♠	♡ J 4 3	♡ 10 2
4 ♠		♢ 9 2	♢ A Q 6 3
		♣ Q 3	♣ A J 7

East bids 2 ♡, intending to play there if West has a weak two in hearts. When West announces spades instead, East makes a game try, which his partner accepts.

West	East	West	East
2 ♢	2 ♡	♠ A J	♠ Q 10 5 3
2NT	3 ♣	♡ A Q 10 3	♡ K 9 8 4
3 ♡	4 ♡	♢ K Q 8 4	♢ J 7 3
		♣ A J 7	♣ 5 2

East seeks a major-suit fit when his partner discloses a balanced 20–22 count.

The 2 ♠ response

This response shows little interest in spades but game possibilities should the opener hold a weak two in hearts. These are the rebids after 2 ♢–2 ♠:

Pass	weak two in spades
2NT, 3 ♣, 3 ♢	as before
3 ♡	weak two in hearts, lower range
3 ♠	weak two in hearts, upper range

This is a common sequence:

West	East	West	East
2 ♢	2 ♠	♠ K Q 10 8 6 5	♠ 7
No		♡ 4	♡ A Q 8 5
		♢ Q 6 4	♢ J 10 8 7 2
		♣ 10 8 3	♣ A K 4

The defence against such hands is difficult.

The 2NT response

This response is conventional and forcing. It must be said early, however, that it is not always strong. The responder will sometimes hold about 9 or 10 points, playable in either major at the three level. It may be good policy then (especially if the fourth player has not passed originally) to bid 2NT defensively. On most occasions, though, the responder who bids 2NT will be looking for game. The opener springs to attention with these rebids:

3 ♣	Weak two in hearts, upper range
3 ♢	Weak two in spades, upper range
3 ♡	Weak two in hearts, lower range
3 ♠	Weak two in spades, lower range
3NT	20–22 balanced
4 ♣	Acol two in clubs
4 ♢	Acol two in diamonds

When the opener indicates a weak two, the responder's next bid is natural at the three level but a cue bid at the four level.

(a)	2 ♢	2NT	Responder holds:	♠ A Q 10 6 5 2
	3 ♣	3 ♠		♡ 9 2
				♢ A J
				♣ A Q 6

Three spades is natural and forcing. If no support is forthcoming, the hand will be playable in 4 ♡.

(b) 2 ◇   2NT   Responder holds: ♠ K Q 6
     3 ♠   4 ♣   ♡ A 10 5
                                        ◇ A Q J 6 2
                                        ♣ A 6

Four clubs is a cue bid, agreeing spades as trumps. In the happy event of the opener showing the diamond king now, a grand slam may result. Note that it would not be sound here for the opener, the long trump hand, to cue-bid a singleton diamond. When the combined playing strength is still being assessed, a cue bid by the long trump hand indicates the ace or king.

Responses at the three level

Three-level responses in a minor are forcing and based on a strong suit:

(a) 2 ◇   3 ♣   Responder holds: ♠ 6
                                        ♡ A J
                                        ◇ A 10 9 4
                                        ♣ A K J 9 6 2

The opener will generally rebid his major at this point (assuming he has a weak two). Over a rebid of 3 ♠ the responder will bid 3NT, leaving partner free to advance to 4 ♣.

Three-level responses in a major are invitational, showing this type of hand:

(b) 2 ◇   3 ♠   Responder holds: ♠ A Q J 8 7 4 2
                                        ♡ 6
                                        ◇ A Q 6
                                        ♣ 10 3

When the second hand intervenes

When the second hand doubles, all responses carry their original meaning. Two new options are available:

Pass   No interest in either major
Redouble   Content to play in 2 $\diamondsuit$ redoubled; at least four
              useful diamonds and some top cards.

Since a pass is available, a response of 2 $\heartsuit$ now carries the
inference of spade support, 2 ♠ of heart support.

				North holds: ♠ K 10 6 2
South	*West*	*North*	*East*	$\heartsuit$ 5 2
2 $\diamondsuit$	dble	2 $\heartsuit$		$\diamondsuit$ A Q 5
				♣ 10 7 6 3

If East now bids a minor at the three level, South will compete
with a spade suit but not with hearts.

When the second hand makes a natural overcall in a suit or
notrumps, all doubles by responder are for penalties. Should the
overcall be in a major suit, the responder may compete on the
assumption that his partner holds the other major:

				North holds: ♠ K 2
South	*West*	*North*	*East*	$\heartsuit$ A 8 5
2 $\diamondsuit$	2 $\heartsuit$	2 ♠		$\diamondsuit$ K Q 8 6
				♣ Q 10 7 4

Here North places his partner with a weak two in spades and
competes accordingly. On a stronger hand he could bid 2NT,
which would keep its conventional meaning.

When the overcall is in a minor suit, *all* bids in hearts by the
responder are a request to play in the opener's major:

				North holds: ♠ A 10 6 4
South	*West*	*North*	*East*	$\heartsuit$ 8 7
2 $\diamondsuit$	3 ♣	3 $\heartsuit$		$\diamondsuit$ A K 10 5 3
				♣ K 5

If South corrects to 3 ♠ now, North will advance to game. If
North had bid 3 ♠ in this sequence, the implication would be that
he could stand 4 $\heartsuit$ (at least).

Defending against the multi-coloured 2 ◇

A common defence to this opening is to pass initially, even on a big hand, and to move into action when the opponents' auction has exhausted itself. We do not advocate this approach. It wastes the first round of bidding and leaves open to doubt whether subsequent action is based on good values or has an element of protection to it. The defence that we suggest is based on some ideas of the British international, Chris Dixon.

Bidding in the second position

The safest entry into the auction is a double. Since the opponents will rarely be in a position to play in two diamonds, the doubler will escape unpunished when he finds his partner with tram tickets. This is the scheme in the second seat:

dble   13–17 fairly flat, or 18+ any shape
2 ♡   13–17 with hearts but at most a doubleton spade
2 ♠   13–17 with spades but at most a doubleton heart
2NT   17–19 with a stop in both majors

All higher bids are natural. Following a double, some interesting points of theory arise:

(a)   *South   West   North   East*   East holds: ♠ 10 8 5
      2 ◇   dble   No   ?   ♡ J 9
                                                    ◇ J 7
                                                    ♣ A 10 9 6 3 2

East need not reply to the double unless he has eight points or so. Here he should pass. If South bids his major and two passes follow, East can compete with three clubs.

(b)   *South   West   North   East*   West holds: ♠ A 10 6
      2 ◇   dble   No   2 ♡   ♡ K Q 9 2
      No   ?   ◇ 8
                                                     ♣ K Q 7 5 2

East has given a 'positive' response to the double, so West is entitled to raise to game.

(c) | *South* | *West* | *North* | *East* | East holds: | ♠ K 10 7 2 |
     | 2 ♢ | dble | 2 ♡ | ? | | ♡ 9 6 4 |
     | | | | | | ♢ A 9 8 3 |
     | | | | | | ♣ Q 5 |

East doubles to show a few bits and pieces. This is a form of responsive double and has no bearing on the major suit that North has chosen to bid. The alternative call of 2 ♠ would be quite unsound, since this might be South's long suit.

Bidding in the fourth position

When the bidding starts 2 ♢–No–2 ♡, the defender in the fourth seat may have the values to enter the auction. This is the scheme:

Double   A takeout double of a weak two in hearts
2 ♠   Natural

Other bids carry the same meaning as in the second seat. With a good hand including a heart suit, the fourth player should pass for the moment.

				East holds:	♠ 6
South	*West*	*North*	*East*		♡ A Q 10 4
2 ♢	No	2 ♡	No		♢ K Q 6 5
					♣ K J 9 3

If the opener rebids two spades, as is likely, East will awake from his slumbers with a second-round takeout double.

When the bidding starts 2 ♢–No–2 ♠, a double by the fourth player is a takeout of a weak two in spades. So the general idea is that you double when you do not want the third player's bid to be passed out. But when the third player bids your suit, you must hold your fire for one round.

Action by the second player on the second round

On some quite good hands it is unsafe—or at any rate inadvisable—to enter until you know which suit the opener holds.

South	West	North	East
2 ◇	No	2 ♡	No
No	?		

West may compete now according to this scheme:

Double	for takeout
2 ♠, 3 ♣, 3 ◇	natural
2NT	both minors

South	West	North	East	West holds: ♠ A J 9 3
2 ◇	No	2 ♡	No	♡ J 9
No	?			◇ J 6 2
				♣ K Q 10 4

It would be unsound for West to enter on the first round. When the opponents subside in two hearts he may compete with a double.

The same method is used when North has responded 2 ♠, but the defenders must be more careful now. A reopening double by West is again for takeout and 2NT shows the minors.

Putting the released bids to good use

Opening bids of 2 ♡ and 2 ♠ will not now be needed to show weak-two hands. Acol players will doubtless use the calls in their traditional roles.

An Acol two bid shows a hand of power and quality. Consider these examples:

(1) ♠ A K Q 10 8 7	(2) ♠ A K 10 6 5	(3) ♠ A K 9 5 4
♡ 2	♡ A Q J 5 4	♡ A 8 7
◇ K Q 4	◇ 7	◇ A 9 5 2
♣ A 10 6	♣ A 3	♣ A

The first hand is a typical Acol two, rich in playing strength. Hand (2) also qualifies for 2 ♠, since partner might easily pass 1 ♠ when there was a game on. The third hand is awkward in the system because an opening 2 ♣ or 2 ♠ might take you too high. The choice is between 1 ♠ and 2 ♣; we would prefer to trust our luck with 2 ♣ rather than risk playing in 1 ♠, withpossibly eleven or twelve tricks on top in a red suit. We have not included a separate chapter on the 2 ♣ opening in this book, as the style is well known, but we will remark here that it is not necessary to play 2 ♣–2 ♢–2 ♠ as unconditionally forcing to game. If responder gives two negative responses, the bidding can be allowed to die in 3 ♠.

The new role for the 2NT opening (a minor two-suiter or a better than average pre-empt in diamonds, hearts or spades) was described in Chapter 5.

SUMMARY

1. A multi-coloured 2 ♢ opening shows:
   (a) a weak two bid in hearts or spades (7–10 points), or
   (b) an Acol two bid in clubs or diamonds, or
   (c) a balanced hand of 20–22 points.
2. A response of 2 ♡ indicates that this is the limit of the hand if the opener has a weak two in hearts. The opener's rebid (if any) specifies his type.
3. A response of 2 ♠ suggests game prospects if opener holds hearts rather than spades.
4. The conventional response on most strong hands is 2NT. The opener then shows his hand type with one of seven possible rebids.
5. Three-level responses in a minor are forcing and based on a strong suit. In a major suit they are invitational, based on a good seven-card suit.

Defending against the multi

6. In the second seat
   dble is 13–17 fairly flat, or 18+ any shape
   2 ♡   is 13–17 with hearts but at most a doubleton spade
   2 ♠   is 13–17 with spades but at most a doubleton heart
   2NT   is 17–19 with both majors stopped

7. The doubler's partner need not respond unless he holds positive values.
8. When the third player bids two of a major over a double, a further double by the fourth player is responsive.
9. After a two-level response in a major, a double by the fourth player is for takeout. With length in the bid major the fourth player should pass initially.

Putting the released bids to use

10. 2 ♡ and 2 ♠ revert to their traditional Acol meaning.
11. 2NT shows a minor two-suiter or a strongish pre-empt in diamonds, hearts or spades (see Chapter 5).
12. After an opening 2 ♣ and a rebid of 2 ♡ or 2 ♠, the bidding may be allowed to die in three of the major when responder shows no sign of life.

Part 2
THE PLAY

12 · Finesse if you must, but . . .

Poor players like finesses—good players don't. But still, there's not always a way round; and it's important to know not only how to finesse but when to finesse. First, consider this innocent-looking holding:

$$\heartsuit \; A \; K \; Q \; 9$$

$$\heartsuit \; 6 \; 5 \; 3$$

You cash $\heartsuit$ A K and East drops the 10 (or jack) on the second round. Do you play for the drop now or finesse the 9? You may be surprised to hear that the finesse is almost twice as likely to gain as laying down the queen. East would play an honour on the second round from 10 x, J x, or J 10 x. It is therefore well with the odds that his second card is from one of the doubleton combinations.

Guess finesses

We shall look first at situations where there is a choice between two finesses (using finesse in the broad sense):

(1) $\diamondsuit$ K J 7   (2) $\diamondsuit$ Q 10 5 2

    $\diamondsuit$ 4 2 $\diamondsuit$ A 6 3

In both cases declarer leads towards the dummy. Assuming West plays low, he must decide which card to play from dummy. Normally the lower card will be the better choice, since this will gain a trick when both honours are onside. But in the second combination declarer should play a low card to the queen if he places the king with West. He will gain when East has J x or J x x, lose only when East has x x.

The timing of a finesse may be vital, as on the following hand:

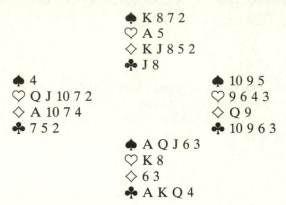

```
              ♠ K 8 7 2
              ♡ A 5
              ◇ K J 8 5 2
              ♣ J 8
♠ 4                          ♠ 10 9 5
♡ Q J 10 7 2                 ♡ 9 6 4 3
◇ A 10 7 4                   ◇ Q 9
♣ 7 5 2                      ♣ 10 9 6 3
              ♠ A Q J 6 3
              ♡ K 8
              ◇ 6 3
              ♣ A K Q 4
```

Both teams in a duplicate match played in six spades from the South side. In one room declarer won the heart lead, drew trumps and cashed his heart and club winners. He then led a diamond towards dummy. West played low and declarer guessed wrongly, playing the jack. East returned a diamond and the slam was one down. Declarer claimed that his line was slightly better than 50 per cent because if East's winning honour had been a singleton he would have had to give a ruff-and-discard.

In the other room declarer won the heart lead in hand and led a diamond at trick 2. This put West to an immediate, and difficult, guess. After a moment's hesitation he played the ace. From his point of view declarer might have had a trump loser and be trying to slip through a singleton diamond. As the play went at the first table, West knew very well that the defence needed two diamond tricks.

(3) ♠ A 10 3   (4) ♠ A 10 5

    ♠ K J 4   ♠ K J 9

With these two holdings declarer can catch the queen in either defender's hand, but he must first guess who holds the queen. A standard ploy on (4) is to lead the jack from hand, hoping to tempt a cover from West. If West plays low without a flicker, declarer goes up with dummy's ace and finesses the 9 on the way back.

(5) ♡ A K 9 2

♡ Q 10 5 4

Tackling the trump suit before he has had much chance to estimate the distribution, declarer leads the ace from dummy. Suppose the 8 falls from one side or the other. Declarer has to consider whether this defender is good enough to have played the 8 from J 8 x x. Suppose, instead, that on the first round only low cards appear. If, say, West is an expert and East is not, declarer may conclude that East is the more likely to hold four trumps.

(6) ◇ A Q 9 6 5 2

◇ K 8 4   ◇ 10

◇ J 7 3

If declarer leads the jack from hand and pins East's 10, he should not expect any congratulations from partner. His play would have cost a trick if West had held the bare king. A low card to the queen would guard against both possibilities. Of course, the jack is right if you intend to play West for K 10 x. This position is similar:

(7) ♣ A K 10 8 6 3

♣ Q   ♣ 9 7 5 4

♣ J 2

Declarer should play a low card to the 10, succeeding when West has the single queen or East the single 9. The general principle is well known: lead low for a finesse unless you are sure you can afford a cover.

Delaying the finesse

It is often right to postpone a key finesse. By ducking a round of the suit first, declarer may find he can drop the outstanding honour or induce a defensive error. This hand illustrates the possibilities:

♠ K 10 9 2
♡ 9 2
♢ A Q 6 3
♣ 8 5 2

♠ Q J 8 4
♡ A K 7
♢ 9 5 4
♣ A K 6

South plays in four spades and the defenders lead two rounds of trumps, both following suit. Declarer should draw the last trump and lead a low diamond from dummy. If East has the king (and not the jack) he may at least give it a look. Assuming the defenders take the trick cheaply, declarer will win the return and cash ♢ A (picking up a possible K x with East). His last shot will be to return to hand and lead a third round of diamonds toward the queen, establishing a trick if West held the king all along. Note that if East holds ♢ K J x x he must play low when the first round of diamonds is led from dummy. Putting in the jack will give declarer the contract.

Combination finesses

Seemingly simple combinations can lead to some interesting tactical battles:

♢ A J 9 5

♢ 7 4 3

Declarer will usually start with a deep finesse of the 9, scoring two tricks if West holds the 10 and one or more of the high honours. It is well known that West should play high from K 10 x or Q 10 x in this situation, particularly when the dummy is short of entries.

The declarer may draw interesting conclusions when an experienced opponent does not insert an honour.

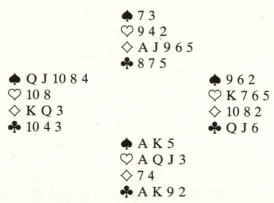

```
                    ♠ 7 3
                    ♡ 9 4 2
                    ◇ A J 9 6 5
                    ♣ 8 7 5
♠ Q J 10 8 4                        ♠ 9 6 2
♡ 10 8                              ♡ K 7 6 5
◇ K Q 3                             ◇ 10 8 2
♣ 10 4 3                            ♣ Q J 6
                    ♠ A K 5
                    ♡ A Q J 3
                    ◇ 7 4
                    ♣ A K 9 2
```

South, playing in 3NT, wins the second round of spades. When he leads a diamond towards dummy, West plays low. Since West would doubtless have played high with K 10 x or Q 10 x, South decides against a deep finesse of the 9. Instead he plays ◇ J, which holds the trick. He is now able to take two heart finesses and make the contract.

This is a frequent combination:

♣ K Q 10

♣ 7 4 2

Declarer starts with a club to the king. East should obviously duck on the first round to give declarer a guess subsequently. When West has ♣ A x x he should be prepared to duck twice.

The defenders must play similarly when the K Q 10 lie in the closed hand. Declarer may sometimes take advantage of this:

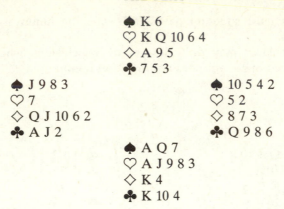

♠ K 6
♥ K Q 10 6 4
◇ A 9 5
♣ 7 5 3

♠ J 9 8 3
♥ 7
◇ Q J 10 6 2
♣ A J 2

♠ 10 5 4 2
♥ 5 2
◇ 8 7 3
♣ Q 9 8 6

♠ A Q 7
♥ A J 9 8 3
◇ K 4
♣ K 10 4

South plays in six hearts and wins the diamond lead. He draws trumps, eliminates diamonds and plays the ace and king of spades. Having set the scene, he plays a club to the king. If West places declarer with 2–5–2–4 shape and ♣ K Q 10 x, he will duck the trick to avoid being endplayed. This deception will not succeed against defenders who signal their suit lengths. An echo in spades by East will enable his partner to count the hand.

When declarer actually does hold K Q 10, the queen is the more likely card to smoke out the ace. As is often the case, though, declarer should vary his play from hand to hand.

The ruffing finesse

In a trump contract declarer has a choice of plays with this holding:

◇ A Q J 8

◇ 5

He can either take a straightforward finesse or play ◇ A and run ◇ Q. When the defenders have already established their tricks, declarer will usually opt for the ruffing finesse. One less trick will be lost should it fail. Sometimes there is no better guide.

Declarer has a chance to be devious with side suits such as these:

(1) ♣ A Q J 6 5   (2) ♣ A Q 8 7 2

    ♣ 8 3   ♣ J 4

If declarer does not mind West taking a trick he may, with the first holding, play ♣ A and return ♣ Q. East, with the king, may not cover. The second holding is similar. Declarer cashes ♣ A and returns a low club. East may hold off his king, concluding that declarer is trying to ruff it out.

Defenders also have their chance in some situations. Here West must give declarer a guess:

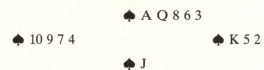

                ♠ A Q 8 6 3

♠ 10 9 7 4   ♠ K 5 2

                ♠ J

South plays ♠ J to the ace and ruffs a low spade. West must drop the 9 or 10 on this trick to lure declarer into playing for a pin on the next round of spades.

This position is similar:

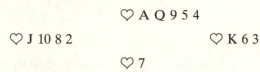

                ♡ A Q 9 5 4

♡ J 10 8 2   ♡ K 6 3

                ♡ 7

West must drop the 10 when declarer takes his first ruff.

East's play on the next hand is fairly well known, though not without its triumphs.

                ◇ K J 10 9 3

◇ 8 5 2   ◇ A Q 7 4

                ◇ 6

Declarer finesses ◇ J. East can tell from his partner's ◇ 2 that declarer has no more diamonds. He therefore wins deceptively with the ace, hoping that declarer will now try to ruff out the queen from West's hand. In the same category is this position:

♣ A Q 10 9 5

♣ 8 7 4 2   ♣ K J

♣ 6 3

If East is marked with the likely strength, he may win the ♣ 10 finesse with the king (the card he is known to hold). Declarer may finesse the 9 on the next round.

Backward finesse and pretended finesse

Declarer has a choice of finesses in this position:

♡ K 6 4

♡ Q 8 7 3   ♡ 10 5 2

♡ A J 9

If he places the queen with West, he should lead ♡ J from hand. It does West no good to cover, obviously. In practice, West is unlikely to cover unless he holds the 10 as well. This consideration may affect declarer's play with this holding:

◇ K 8 3

◇ A J 7 4

When entries to dummy are scarce, not much is lost by leading ◇ J from hand. West won't cover with Q x x.

Combinations of this type are much the same:

◇ Q 7 2

◇ K 10 8 5

Leading ◇ 10 from hand is not much inferior. West won't cover from J x x or A J x x.

The intra-finesse

The Brazilian maestro, Gabriel Chagas, added to the language when he invented the term 'intra-finesse'. The positions he had in mind were not new, of course, but had received little attention in bridge literature. Declarer needs to play this suit for one loser:

♠ Q 9 3 2

♠ 10 6   ♠ K J 7

♠ A 8 5 4

He starts by finessing dummy's 9, losing to the knave. Subsequently the queen is led from dummy, trapping East's king and pinning West's 10. Note that when declarer can place East with the king, the intra-finesse is a better bet than playing for the drop on the second round. An initial holding of K J x is more likely than K J alone. Similar conclusions can be drawn here:

♡ A 8 3

♡ J 4   ♡ Q 10 7 5

♡ K 9 6 2

Declarer finesses dummy's 8, losing to the 10. When the ace subsequently drops West's knave, the 'principle of restricted choice' applies: *It is more likely that a defender had no choice in his play of a card than that he selected it from two cards of equal rank*. With this holding, then, declarer should finesse the 9 on the third round. East can worry declarer by winning the first round with the queen—a play that can hardly cost.

The obligatory finesse

This is the name given to a situation where declarer appears to have only one chance to make the maximum number of tricks: he must play for a particular honour card to fall.

◇ Q 8 6 3

◇ A 9   ◇ J 10 5

◇ K 7 4 2

When a diamond to the queen holds, declarer leads a second

round of the suit and plays low from hand. West's ace beats the air. There are many similar plays. For example:

             ◇ J 8 7 2

◇ A 10 3   ◇ K 9

             ◇ Q 6 5 4

If it is reasonable to suppose that West would have led a diamond from a holding headed by A K, declarer should begin with a low card to the queen. This will be an immediate success when East holds both honours. Should the queen lose to West's ace or king, declarer's best chance is to duck the second round, playing for the other honour to be bare.

The Chinese finesse

At the beginning of the play declarer usually knows more about the general situation than the defenders. Bold deceptions may succeed that would stand much less chance later in the play:

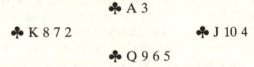

             ♣ A 3

♣ K 8 7 2   ♣ J 10 4

            ♣ Q 9 6 5

Seeing no hope of an endplay, declarer leads ♣ Q from hand at an early stage. West may hold off, placing declarer with Q J 9 or Q J 10. This piece of skulduggery is known as the Chinese finesse. Since West is likely to cover when he holds K 10, the manoeuvre has extra chance of success when declarer holds the 10 himself.

13 · To cover or not to cover?

Every bridge player hears at an early stage that it is good form to 'cover an honour with an honour'. Failure to do so, he is told, is almost as bad as revoking. In fact, more tricks are surrendered by ill-advised covering than by failing to cover.

The decisions involved are often difficult. When caught unawares, it is usually better *not* to cover, because declarer will then often have alternative plays. The purpose of covering is to promote lower cards in one's own or one's partner's hand. Everyone knows this situation:

$$\heartsuit \text{ A J 6}$$

$$\heartsuit \text{ K 7 4 3} \qquad \heartsuit \text{ 10 8 2}$$

$$\heartsuit \text{ Q 9 5}$$

When West covers South's lead of the queen, he promotes his partner's 10.

$$\diamondsuit \text{ A 10 3}$$

$$\diamondsuit \text{ K 6 4} \qquad \diamondsuit \text{ Q 9 7 5}$$

$$\diamondsuit \text{ J 8 2}$$

Similarly, here, West's cover of the jack promotes his partner's Q 9.

There are two general rules that will assist the defender on most occasions.

Rule 1: When declarer leads an honour from hand, cover if the dummy holds two honours over you.

Rule 2: Cover an honour led from dummy unless it is one of touching honours.

It can be seen that these two rules complement each other. On the two examples given above, Rule 1 would apply if South were declarer. If North were declarer, Rule 2 would be followed.

Let us look first at some of the frequent situations in which 'covering an honour with an honour' would cost a trick.

Case 1. A subsequent trick is established for declarer.

♠ A 7 5

♠ K 9 8 2   ♠ Q 6 4

♠ J 10 3

If West innocently covers the knave with his king, declarer will easily establish a second trick. Rule 1 indicates that West was wrong to cover.

♣ Q J 9

♣ 10 6 3   ♣ K 8 5 2

♣ A 7 4

Again, if East (contrary to Rule 2) covers the queen with the king, it will cost his side a trick.

Even if East holds K x there is no necessity to cover:

♦ Q J 9 6

♦ 10 7 4   ♦ K 2

♦ A 8 5 3

If East allows dummy's queen to pass, declarer will have a choice of plays on the next round. Note that West, after East's play of the 2, can give declarer a push in the wrong direction by dropping the 7 on the first round, creating the impression that he holds 10 7 doubleton. However, as with most false cards, this play loses its effect if the defender *always* plays the middle card from 10 x x. Declarer can then draw a new set of inferences.

Case 2. Declarer is saved a guess.

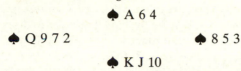

♠ A 6 4

♠ Q 9 7 2   ♠ 8 5 3

♠ K J 10

When the jack is led, West should play low (Rule 1). There is a chance that declarer will put on dummy's ace and finesse the 10 on the way back. The next situation is less clear because two honours lie in the dummy:

♠ A 10 5

♠ Q 8 2   ♠ 7 6 4

♠ K J 9 3

When the jack is led, it is probably wrong to cover despite Rule 1. Declarer is, after all, unlikely to broach the suit in this way if he holds J x x or J x x x. This would cost him a trick if West held a doubleton honour and covered the jack.

On the following hand declarer is playing in six spades and has a choice of finesses.

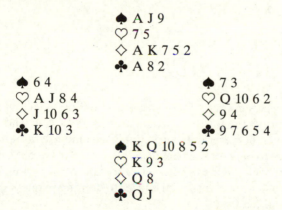

♠ A J 9
♡ 7 5
♢ A K 7 5 2
♣ A 8 2

♠ 6 4   ♠ 7 3
♡ A J 8 4   ♡ Q 10 6 2
♢ J 10 6 3   ♢ 9 4
♣ K 10 3   ♣ 9 7 6 5 4

♠ K Q 10 8 5 2
♡ K 9 3
♢ Q 8
♣ Q J

West leads a trump, taken in hand. Declarer sees that if diamonds divide 3–3 he will be able to discard all his hearts and take a club finesse for the overtrick. On the more likely 4–2 diamond division, however, he will have to guess whether to discard two hearts and rely on the club finesse or to discard a club and hope that ♡ A is well placed.

The artful declarer will lead ♣ Q from hand at trick 2. Should West be so unwise as to cover this card, or if he is caught napping and ponders before playing low, declarer is bound to succeed. If West follows smoothly with a low card, declarer will doubtless rise with dummy's ace. He will then draw trumps and test the diamonds, discarding the club loser. When the diamonds fail to divide he will end lamely with a losing finesse in hearts.

Case 3. Declarer is saved an entry.

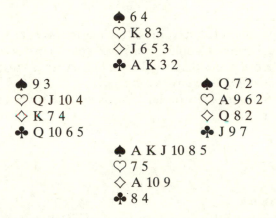

South plays in four spades and the defenders attack in hearts. Declarer ruffs the third round and crosses to ♣ A to lead ♢ J. If East covers, declarer will win with the ace and use his remaining club entry to pick up the trumps. He can then drive out ♢ K and claim ten tricks. If East allows ♢ J to run to his partner's king, declarer will have insufficient entries to dummy to finesse in both spades and diamonds.

How can East tell whether to cover ♢ J ? Even if he considers the diamond suit in isolation, he should reason that declarer is unlikely to hold A 10 x or K 10 x. With such a holding he would have led a low diamond from the dummy.

Case 4. Holding off gives declarer a losing option.

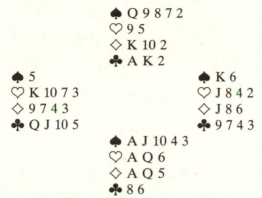

♠ Q 9 8 7 2
♡ 9 5
◇ K 10 2
♣ A K 2

♠ 5
♡ K 10 7 3
◇ 9 7 4 3
♣ Q J 10 5

♠ K 6
♡ J 8 4 2
◇ J 8 6
♣ 9 7 4 3

♠ A J 10 4 3
♡ A Q 6
◇ A Q 5
♣ 8 6

South plays in six spades and wins the ♣ Q lead on the table. He now leads dummy's ♠ Q.

If East covers, declarer has twelve top tricks. Should East hold off the king, declarer may well decide to rise with the ace, eliminate the minor suits, and exit in trumps.

It is not difficult to hold off here. To cover would gain only if declarer's trump holding were as meagre as A 10 x x. Apart from the actual situation, declarer might hold ♠ A J 10 x x x and have no intention of running the queen. Remember that the object of covering is to promote a lower card in your partner's hand or your own.

Case 5. The defenders clash their honours.

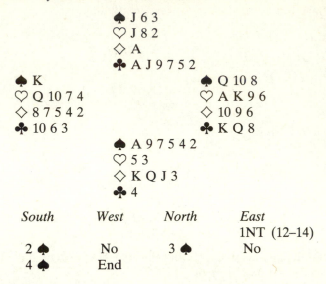

	♠ J 6 3		
	♡ J 8 2		
	◇ A		
	♣ A J 9 7 5 2		

♠ K		♠ Q 10 8
♡ Q 10 7 4		♡ A K 9 6
◇ 8 7 5 4 2		◇ 10 9 6
♣ 10 6 3		♣ K Q 8

	♠ A 9 7 5 4 2	
	♡ 5 3	
	◇ K Q J 3	
	♣ 4	

South	West	North	East
			1NT (12–14)
2 ♠	No	3 ♠	No
4 ♠	End		

The defenders play on hearts and declarer ruffs the third round. He must try now to escape for one trump loser. Normal play is the ace followed by a low card to the jack, winning when the spades are 2–2 or East holds a singleton honour. In this case the opening bid precludes the second possibility, so declarer crosses to ◇ A and leads ♠ J from the dummy.

Should East cover with his queen, declarer's ace and West's king will complete a star-studded first round of trumps. Declarer will cross to ♣ A and lead towards ♠ 9, losing only one trump.

Covering when holding a doubleton honour

The two basic rules given at the start of this chapter (cover declarer's honour if dummy holds two honours; and cover dummy's honour unless it's one of touching honours) must often be flaunted when the defender's honour is doubleton. If he declines to cover on the first round, he may have to play the high card on thin air when the next lead is made.

$\heartsuit$ Q J 4

$\heartsuit$ 9 6 5 3 $\heartsuit$ K 7

$\heartsuit$ A 10 8 2

If East does not cover when the queen is led, declarer will run the queen and probably continue with the 4 from dummy. All four tricks will be made. Covering the queen will bring West's 9 into play. These situations are tricky, though. As we saw before, if declarer's holding were headed by the A 9 8, covering the queen would save him a guess.

$\clubsuit$ J 10 2

$\clubsuit$ A 8 6 3 $\clubsuit$ Q 5

$\clubsuit$ K 9 7 4

Here East should cover dummy's lead of $\clubsuit$ J. West's $\clubsuit$ 8 will then guard the fourth round of the suit. Covering will gain also when South has $\clubsuit$ A K x x.

If North were the closed hand, East would have a difficult decision. North might hold $\clubsuit$ A J 10 and be fishing for the queen. East must plan his play in advance.

Covering when two honours are held

The rules are different when the defender himself holds two honours.

$\spadesuit$ K 8 6

$\spadesuit$ A Q 7 $\spadesuit$ 9 5 4

$\spadesuit$ J 10 3 2

When the declarer leads the jack or 10 from hand, West must cover to ensure two tricks for the defence.

$\diamondsuit$ 10 9 5

$\diamondsuit$ A 8 3 2 $\diamondsuit$ Q J 6

$\diamondsuit$ K 7 4

Similarly, East must cover dummy's 10 (or 9) to prevent declarer establishing a trick in the suit.

It is often right to cover cards well below honour rank:

$\clubsuit$ K 10 2

$\clubsuit$ Q 9 5 $\clubsuit$ A J 6 3

$\clubsuit$ 8 7 4

If West allows declarer's $\clubsuit$ 7 to pass, it will force East's jack. Declarer will subsequently finesse dummy's 10, thereby stealing a trick. West must cover the 7, and on the next round the 8.

Covering to avoid an endplay

Generally speaking, when you hold a *lot* of good cards in defence, you should cover in the hope that part of the load can be transferred to your partner.

$\spadesuit$ K 9 6
$\heartsuit$ Q J 4
$\diamondsuit$ K 8 2
$\clubsuit$ A K Q 2

$\spadesuit$ 7 5 3 $\spadesuit$ 10 8 2
$\heartsuit$ 10 8 5 2 $\heartsuit$ K 7 3
$\diamondsuit$ J 10 9 3 $\diamondsuit$ Q 6 5
$\clubsuit$ 8 5 $\clubsuit$ J 10 6 4

$\spadesuit$ A Q J 4
$\heartsuit$ A 9 6
$\diamondsuit$ A 7 4
$\clubsuit$ 9 7 3

South plays in 6NT and wins the $\diamondsuit$ J lead in hand. He crosses to a club and leads $\heartsuit$ Q from dummy. If East fails to cover this card, he will eventually be thrown in on the fourth round of clubs to lead away from $\heartsuit$ K.

14 · Strip for action

Throw-in plays are slippery creatures that often evade declarer's net. The defender you have craftily reduced to ♡ A ♣ K x has a nasty habit of finding a second heart when you put him in. Even when your throw-in succeeds, the finesse you avoid is nearly always onside.

There is one type of throw-in play that is relatively easy to perform. The reason why it is called *elimination play* is that certain suits are eliminated from both hands before the defender is put on lead. Provided declarer has at least one trump in each hand, the return of an eliminated suit will concede a ruff-and-discard. To avoid this, the defender may decide to open a new suit, often to declarer's advantage. This is an elementary example of elimination play:

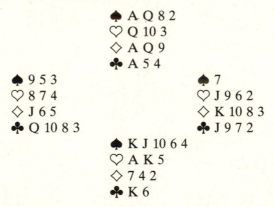

♠ A Q 8 2
♡ Q 10 3
◇ A Q 9
♣ A 5 4

♠ 9 5 3
♡ 8 7 4
◇ J 6 5
♣ Q 10 8 3

♠ 7
♡ J 9 6 2
◇ K 10 8 3
♣ J 9 7 2

♠ K J 10 6 4
♡ A K 5
◇ 7 4 2
♣ K 6

West leads a club against six spades. Declarer wins and pulls three rounds of trumps. He then plays ♣ A and ruffs a club (eliminating the clubs). Next he cashes three rounds of hearts, ending in hand (eliminating the hearts). Now comes a diamond to the 9. East wins with the 10 and considers the unattractive alternatives open to him. A heart or club return will give a ruff-and-discard. A diamond return will run into dummy's A Q.

With this diamond holding declarer was sure of success, however the defenders' cards lay. An important defensive point arises when declarer's exit suit is slightly weaker:

$$\diamond \text{ A Q 8}$$

$$\diamond \text{ J 6 5} \qquad \qquad \diamond \text{ K 10 9 3}$$

$$\diamond \text{ 7 4 2}$$

When declarer tries to execute the throw-in, West must insert ◇ J. Whether declarer covers or not, he will now lose two diamond tricks. This is a similar position where the defender in the second seat must be alert:

$$\clubsuit \text{ K 9 7}$$

$$\clubsuit \text{ Q 5 4} \qquad \qquad \clubsuit \text{ A J 10 2}$$

$$\clubsuit \text{ 8 6 3}$$

Declarer has eliminated the other two side suits and now leads a club from hand. If the defenders need three tricks from the suit to break the contract, West must climb boldly with his queen. If West plays a low card, declarer will duck the trick to East and claim the contract.

These second-hand-high plays are equally important when declarer is leading towards the closed hand. A defender must be particularly wary of doubleton honour holdings:

$$\spadesuit \text{ 8 7 4}$$

$$\spadesuit \text{ A J 9 5 2} \qquad \qquad \spadesuit \text{ K 6}$$

$$\spadesuit \text{ Q 10 3}$$

When a low spade is led from dummy, East must play the king whenever three tricks are needed. Playing low will cost a trick when South has an elimination ending. Singleton aces and kings are a special hazard, in the trump suit as well as in the side suits.

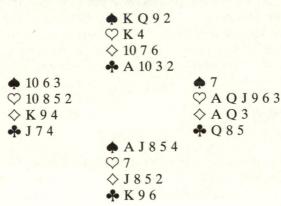

```
                    ♠ A 7
                    ♡ 8 5 3
                    ◇ A 10 8 7 4
                    ♣ 7 6 2
  ♠ Q 8 6 3                        ♠ 10 9 5 2
  ♡ A K Q J 4                      ♡ 10 7 6 2
  ◇ K                              ◇ Q 6
  ♣ Q 9 4                          ♣ 10 5 3
                    ♠ K J 4
                    ♡ 9
                    ◇ J 9 5 3 2
                    ♣ A K J 8
```

South opens 1 ◇ and West doubles. Chasing a vulnerable game, always a worthy cause, South eventually arrives in 5 ◇. West leads ♡ A. If he makes the seemingly obvious continuation of another heart, South will eliminate the major suits and duck the first round of trumps when West's king appears. To prevent this minor tragedy, West should switch to ◇ K at trick 2. Declarer will doubtless proceed with his elimination, but when he exits in trumps East can safely play a club.

It is easy for East to play too quickly on this type of hand:

```
                    ♠ K Q 9 2
                    ♡ K 4
                    ◇ 10 7 6
                    ♣ A 10 3 2
  ♠ 10 6 3                         ♠ 7
  ♡ 10 8 5 2                       ♡ A Q J 9 6 3
  ◇ K 9 4                          ◇ A Q 3
  ♣ J 7 4                          ♣ Q 8 5
                    ♠ A J 8 5 4
                    ♡ 7
                    ◇ J 8 5 2
                    ♣ K 9 6
```

South plays in 3 ♠ after East has opened the bidding in hearts. West leads ♡ 2 to East's jack. A lazy heart continuation will end the defence. South will ruff, draw trumps and exit in diamonds. The defenders will then have to broach the club suit and declarer will play for split honours.

Since the ♡ 2 lead might well be from a four-card suit, East should switch to ♢ Q at the second trick. The defenders will take their three diamond tricks and exit with ♡ A. Eventually a club trick will come their way.

Declarer will often spurn a finesse in favour of an elimination play:

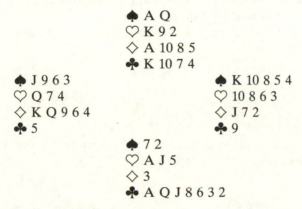

South plays in six clubs and wins the ♢ K lead in dummy. He now ruffs a diamond high, crosses to ♣ K and ruffs another diamond. Crossing once more in trumps, he ruffs dummy's last diamond, eliminating the suit. He now sees that if the spade finesse is right there is no need to take it; ace and queen will be good enough. When South adopts this line, East wins and must play hearts, giving declarer a double chance.

When a defender is obliged to open a new suit, the choice of card may be critical. These are common positions:

♣ A 9 2

♣ Q 7 6 4   ♣ J 8 3

♣ K 10 5

If West exits with a low club, the most kind-hearted of declarers will have no option but to play for divided honours. If West has the wit to play ♣ Q, declarer may decide to win with the king and play West for Q J x.

When West is known to be a competent defender it is well with the odds to play for divided honours in this situation. Declarer's best shot is therefore to win an honour from West in the dummy and finesse against East on the way back.

From J 9 x or Q 9 x it may be essential for West to play the honour:

◇ K 10 4

◇ J 9 5   ◇ Q 6 3 2

◇ A 8 7

The jack is the only card to foil declarer. An interesting corollary arises on these holdings:

◇ K 10 3

◇ Q J 5 2   ◇ 9 7 4

◇ A 8 6

If West exits with ◇ 2 declarer may be tempted to play low from dummy, gaining if West has led from Q 9 or J 9. This is a flimsy argument in a game of good standard. With Q 9 x or J 9 x West would have led his honour. In the above situation, then, declarer should play dummy's 10.

In the next position East is on lead and the defenders need three tricks from the suit:

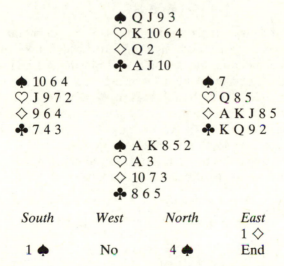

♠ 10 8 3

♠ A J 4 ♠ Q 9 6 2

♠ K 7 5

East exits with ♠ Q (best). If declarer places him with Q J 9, he will play low from hand to force a continuation away from ♠ J. If declarer makes the more likely play of covering with the king, West will win with the ace and return ♠ 4. Declarer may go wrong now by inserting dummy's 8.

Sometimes declarer cannot achieve a perfect elimination. Lack of trumps or entries may make it impossible to eliminate one of the side suits. He may even have to leave a trump outstanding. In such cases declarer must hope that no safe exit card lies with the defender who is to be thrown in. This type of play is known as a *partial elimination*. See how it works on this hand:

```
              ♠ Q J 9 3
              ♡ K 10 6 4
              ◇ Q 2
              ♣ A J 10
 ♠ 10 6 4                    ♠ 7
 ♡ J 9 7 2                   ♡ Q 8 5
 ◇ 9 6 4                     ◇ A K J 8 5
 ♣ 7 4 3                     ♣ K Q 9 2
              ♠ A K 8 5 2
              ♡ A 3
              ◇ 10 7 3
              ♣ 8 6 5
```

South	West	North	East
			1 ◇
1 ♠	No	4 ♠	End

West leads ◇ 9 and East plays three rounds of the suit, declarer ruffing in the dummy. Declarer sees that if trumps are 2–2 he will be able to eliminate hearts and have a certain end-play in clubs. He ruffs the third round of hearts and plays the queen and ace of trumps. On this occasion the trump suit fails to oblige. Leaving one trump outstanding, declarer finesses ♣ J. East wins and has no good return.

Guile as well as technique is required on a hand of this type:

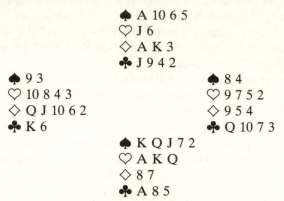

Declarer plays in six spades and wins the diamond lead in dummy. If he plays in straightforward fashion now (drawing trumps, eliminating the red suits and playing ace and another club), the most somnolent of Wests may see the need to unblock ♣ K. Instead, South should cross to ♣ A at trick 2, as though about to finesse in trumps. There is a better chance now that West will retain his ♣ K; wrongly, of course, for the one certainty is that South does not hold ♣ A Q.

Having made this point, it is only fair to observe that declarer can double-cross the defender on his left:

♣ J 9 7 2

♣ K 8   ♣ 10 6 5 3

♣ A Q 4

If declarer places the king with West he may try the effect of laying down the ace at an early stage. Fearing an end play, West may unblock the king.

The defenders must sacrifice two honour cards to beat this slam:

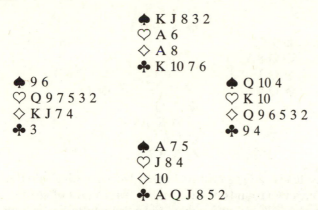

```
                    ♠ K J 8 3 2
                    ♡ A 6
                    ♢ A 8
                    ♣ K 10 7 6
♠ 9 6                                    ♠ Q 10 4
♡ Q 9 7 5 3 2                            ♡ K 10
♢ K J 7 4                                ♢ Q 9 6 5 3 2
♣ 3                                      ♣ 9 4
                    ♠ A 7 5
                    ♡ J 8 4
                    ♢ 10
                    ♣ A Q J 8 5 2
```

West finds a heart lead against six clubs and declarer wins the trick with dummy's ace. If East fails to unblock ♡ K, West's excellent lead will be wasted. Declarer will draw trumps, eliminate diamonds and exit to East's bare ♡ K.

An unblock by East at trick 1 is only part of the defence needed to beat this contract. This will be the lie of the hearts when declarer exits in the suit:

```
                    ♡ 6

♡ Q 9 7 3 2                    ♡ 10

                    ♡ J 8
```

South leads ♡ 8 from hand. West must rise with the queen to save East from the end play. This play, where a defender opens his jaws to swallow partner's high card, is known as the *Crocodile Coup*.

Finally, there is the 'plastic elimination play':

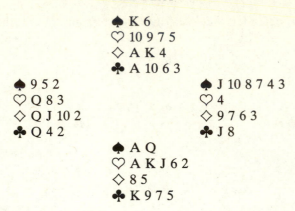

West leads ◇ Q against six hearts. Declarer wins with the ace and takes two rounds of trumps and two rounds of spades. He then plays ◇ K and ruffs a diamond before putting West on play with a trump.

An inexperienced player in the West seat would probably exit with a low club. A slightly better player might push out ♣ Q, hoping to put declarer to a guess.

A defender who has counted declarer for a 2–5–2–4 distribution will exit with a diamond or a spade, giving a ruff-and-discard. This may earn a sharp glance from partner —but it will also break the contract.

15 · Er . . . who's on lead?

The skilled declarer moves smoothly backwards and forwards between his hand and the dummy, rather like a snooker player compiling a break. This process is eased by various tricks of the trade. A common manoeuvre is to win a trick with a higher card than necessary to create an entry to dummy:

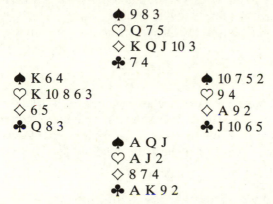

South plays in 3NT and captures the heart lead with the ace rather than the jack. East wins the third round of diamonds, but on any return South can establish ♡ Q as an entry to the long suit.

Similarly, the declarer may jettison a high card to create an entry to the opposite hand:

♠ J 5 3
♡ K Q 10 3
◇ J 9 6
♣ 9 7 5

♠ Q 10 8 4 2   ♠ A 7 6
♡ J 7 6   ♡ A 9 4 2
◇ 4   ◇ K 8 3
♣ J 8 4 2   ♣ Q 10 3

♠ K 9
♡ 8 5
◇ A Q 10 7 5 2
♣ A K 6

Against 3NT West leads ♠ 4 to his partner's ace. Declarer unblocks the king! If the defenders persist with spades, dummy's jack will serve as an entry for a winning diamond finesse. If they switch to clubs instead, declarer will have time to establish a heart entry to dummy. It is strange to note that East can scuttle the contract by playing low at trick 1.

That simple fellow, the finesse, often provides an extra entry:

(1) ◇ K 10 2   (2) ◇ A 10 5

     ◇ A Q 6   ◇ K J 7

In both these positions declarer can try for a second entry by finessing ◇ 10. Learned Wests are supposed to scotch this plan by inserting their honour, but it rarely happens. Declarer can make sure it doesn't happen with this holding:

♣ A 10 4

♣ J 9 6 3 2   ♣ K 8

♣ Q 7 5

West leads ♣ 3 to his partner's king. By unblocking the queen from hand, declarer makes sure of two entries to dummy.

When there is a 4–4 fit in a suit, a familiar technique is to conjure extra entries by overtaking high cards:

♡ A J 5 2

♡ K Q 10 4

Declarer cashes the king and then overtakes the queen with dummy's ace. If the suit breaks 3–2 he can later overtake his 10 with the jack, establishing the 5 as a third entry to dummy.

There is a pretty deceptive play based on this theme. It must be admitted that it occurs more often in the bridge writer's sanctum than at the card table:

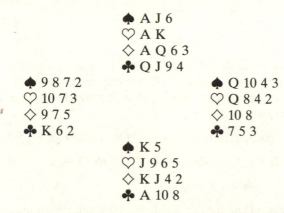

♠ A J 6
♡ A K
♢ A Q 6 3
♣ Q J 9 4

♠ 9 8 7 2
♡ 10 7 3
♢ 9 7 5
♣ K 6 2

♠ Q 10 4 3
♡ Q 8 4 2
♢ 10 8
♣ 7 5 3

♠ K 5
♡ J 9 6 5
♢ K J 4 2
♣ A 10 8

South opens a 12–14 notrump and plays in 6NT, West finding the troublesome spade lead. Declarer wins with the king and plays ♢ 4 to dummy's queen. The club finesse loses and West continues his unwelcome attack on the spade suit.

Declarer wins in dummy and cashes his top cards in hearts and clubs. After playing ♢ 6 to the king, he overtakes ♢ J with the ace. This is the carefully contrived end position:

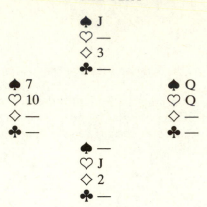

Declarer leads ◇ 3 from dummy. If East missed the early diamond pips, he will discard the wrong queen now.

When dummy is short of entries the defenders must take active steps to keep it that way:

(1)   ♣ A J 10 6 2   (2)   ♣ A J 9 5 4

   ♣ Q 8 5   ♣ K 7   ♣ Q 10 2   ♣ K 6

        ♣ 9 4 3   ♣ 8 7 3

If dummy has no entry outside the club suit, West must insert ♣ Q in both these positions. Even when declarer has three small clubs, as here, he can scarcely risk releasing ♣ A on either of the first two rounds. The defenders will score two tricks.

Declarer makes the same play in this well-known position:

```
                    ♠ Q 10 5
                    ♡ J 7
                    ◇ A K Q 10 6 5
                    ♣ K 9
♠ 8 4                                   ♠ A J 9 7 2
♡ A 6 4 3 2                             ♡ 10 8 5
◇ 9 4                                   ◇ 8 3
♣ 7 6 5 3                               ♣ A 10 2
                    ♠ K 6 3
                    ♡ K Q 9
                    ◇ J 7 2
                    ♣ Q J 8 4
```

South	West	North	East
		1 ◇	1 ♠
2NT	No	3NT	

West leads ♠ 8 and the queen is played from dummy. East must win and cannot safely continue the suit.

Declarer may consider a deceptive play on a slightly different lie of the spade suit:

```
              ♠ Q 10 5

♠ 9 8 4                    ♠ A J 7 6 2

              ♠ K 3
```

West leads ♠ 9 against a notrump contract. If West is likely to gain the lead later, declarer should play ♠ Q at trick 1. East may read his partner for a doubleton and not risk a continuation of the suit.

Plays of the same type are available to the defenders. Here they attack dummy's entries in preference to establishing their own long suit:

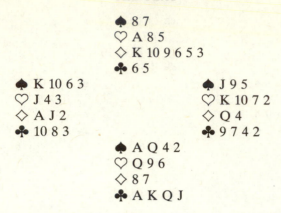

Playing in 3NT, declarer wins the spade lead and finesses ♢ 10 to East's queen. A spade return now would prove too slow; declarer would establish the diamonds. Instead, East switches to ♡ K. If declarer ducks to preserve his entry, East will switch back to spades. East's play of an unsupported honour to remove an entry is known as the *Merrimac Coup*.

A closely related play is used to force an entry to partner's hand:

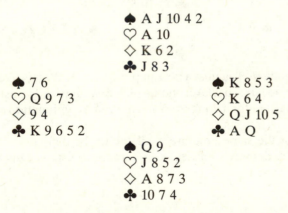

West leads ♣ 5 against 1NT. East wins with the ace and cashes the queen. South is marked with ♢ A, so East's best chance of reaching partner's hand is in hearts. At trick 3 he switches to ♡ K. Whether or not declarer takes the trick, East can eventually cross to his partner's ♡ Q when in with the spade king. This is a true example of the *Deschapelles Coup*, a title loosely attributed to various sacrificial plays.

Another spectacular technique is that of the unblocking discard:

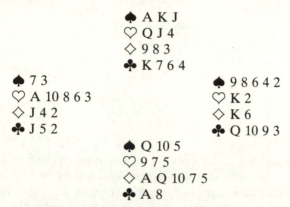

```
              ♠ A K J
              ♡ Q J 4
              ◇ 9 8 3
              ♣ K 7 6 4
♠ 7 3                          ♠ 9 8 6 4 2
♡ A 10 8 6 3                   ♡ K 2
◇ J 4 2                        ◇ K 6
♣ J 5 2                        ♣ Q 10 9 3
              ♠ Q 10 5
              ♡ 9 7 5
              ◇ A Q 10 7 5
              ♣ A 8
```

Against 3NT West leads ♡ 6 to his partner's king. East's ♡ 2 return proclaims an original doubleton, so West sees no profit in holding off his ace. When he wins and returns a third round of the suit, East discards ◇ K, hoping this will create an entry to partner's hand. Declarer has little option but to play three rounds of diamonds and the contract goes one down. If East had retained ◇ K, declarer would have led twice towards his diamonds, ducking when the king appeared.

Declarer's main weapon in the communications battle is the hold-up play. Although the defenders will frequently have to submit, there is one type of hand on which they can defuse the weapon:

```
              ♠ 5 2
              ♡ A Q 9
              ◇ Q 10 9 7 4 2
              ♣ A 8
♠ 7 4                         ♠ K Q 10 8 6 3
♡ 10 8 4 3                    ♡ 5 2
◇ K 5 3                       ◇ A 6
♣ J 9 5 2                     ♣ Q 7 4
              ♠ A J 9
              ♡ K J 7 6
              ◇ J 8
              ♣ K 10 6 3
```

South	West	North	East
		1 ◇	1 ♠
3NT			

West leads ♣ 7. If East plays a high honour, declarer will duck and make the contract easily since West will be out of spades when he takes his diamond honour. Instead, East should play ♠ 10 at trick 1, forcing declarer to part with a stopper. Now West can clear the spade suit when he wins ◇ K.

It is sometimes right for declarer to release his high card earlier than necessary in an attempt to block the enemy's suit:

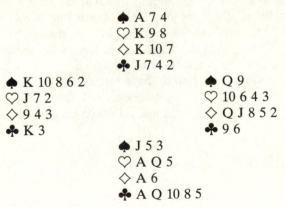

```
              ♠ A 7 4
              ♡ K 9 8
              ◇ K 10 7
              ♣ J 7 4 2
♠ K 10 8 6 2                  ♠ Q 9
♡ J 7 2                       ♡ 10 6 4 3
◇ 9 4 3                       ◇ Q J 8 5 2
♣ K 3                         ♣ 9 6
              ♠ J 5 3
              ♡ A Q 5
              ◇ A 6
              ♣ A Q 10 8 5
```

West leads ♠ 6 against 3NT. Since the key finesse is into West's hand, it is futile to hold up the spade ace, and to play low from dummy will gain only if West has led from K Q. So declarer goes up with the ace on the first trick. The club finesse loses but the spade suit is now blocked.

The same play may succeed on holdings like these:

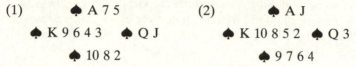

(1)   ♠ A 7 5   (2)   ♠ A J

♠ K 9 6 4 3 ♠ Q J   ♠ K 10 8 5 2 ♠ Q 3

       ♠ 10 8 2   ♠ 9 7 6 4

In both cases declarer prevents the run of the suit by playing dummy's ace at trick 1.

A few rubbers to the good after these handy blocking plays, declarer may find himself in a suit contract where the Machiavellian defenders are plotting a ruff. No matter; he may be able to outwit them by exchanging one trick for another.

                   ♠ A 10 7
                   ♡ J 8 2
                   ♢ J 5
                   ♣ A K Q 8 3

♠ 5   ♠ K 8 3
♡ 7 6 5 3   ♡ K 10 9 4
♢ Q 10 4 2   ♢ A K 8 7 3
♣ 10 9 6 5   ♣ 2

                   ♠ Q J 9 6 4 2
                   ♡ A Q
                   ♢ 9 6
                   ♣ J 7 4

South	*West*	*North*	*East*
		1 ♣	dble
1 ♠	No	2 ♠	No
4 ♠	End		

West leads ♢ 2 to his partner's king and East switches to ♣ 2. The bidding and the early defence paint a clear picture. When

East is in with the trump king he will cross to his partner's $\diamond$ Q and obtain a club ruff.

Declarer must aim to cut the link to West's hand. He wins the club switch in the dummy and finesses $\heartsuit$ Q successfully. He then cashes $\heartsuit$ A and crosses to the ace of trumps to play $\heartsuit$ J. East has to win the trick and South hastily discards his remaining diamond, making the contract safe. By exchanging the defenders' diamond trick for a heart trick, declarer denies them their ruff. This technique, being a cut above the ordinary run of play, is known as the *Scissors Coup*.

16 · Magic in the trump suit

A notrump contract often turns into a straightforward race between declarer and the defenders, the result depending on who is first to knock out the other side's stoppers and cash the requisite number of tricks. In a suit contract the possible lines of play are more varied and colourful. There are numerous tactical possibilities for both declarer and the defenders.

First we look at some of the stratagems available to declarer.

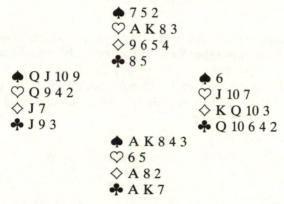

```
                    ♠ 7 5 2
                    ♡ A K 8 3
                    ◇ 9 6 5 4
                    ♣ 8 5
  ♠ Q J 10 9                        ♠ 6
  ♡ Q 9 4 2                         ♡ J 10 7
  ◇ J 7                             ◇ K Q 10 3
  ♣ J 9 3                           ♣ Q 10 6 4 2
                    ♠ A K 8 4 3
                    ♡ 6 5
                    ◇ A 8 2
                    ♣ A K 7
```

South plays in four spades and West leads the queen of trumps. South wins and cashes a second round of trumps, discovering the bad break. He now has two trump losers and two unavoidable diamond losers. One down? Let us see.

Declarer cashes dummy's two heart honours and ruffs a heart in hand. Then he plays ♣ A K and ruffs a club in dummy. When he ruffs dummy's last heart in hand, West has to follow suit. Declarer has now scored ten tricks—five side-suit winners, two top trumps, one ruff in dummy and two ruffs in hand.

If the other defender, East, had held ♠ Q J 10 9, the play

would have followed a similar course. After a heart ruff in hand and a club ruff in the dummy, this would be the ending:

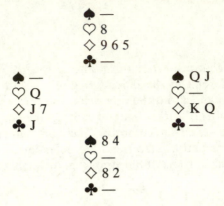

Declarer leads the last heart from dummy and will score one of his low trumps whether East ruffs or not. This play is known as the *coup en passant*.

Sometimes declarer holds a trump tenace over East but cannot finesse in the usual way because dummy's trumps are exhausted. This is a typical example:

```
                    ♠ K 6
                    ♡ A 8 6 3
                    ◇ A 8 5
                    ♣ A Q J 2
    ♠ 4                           ♠ Q 8 7 3
    ♡ Q 10 9 7 4                  ♡ K J 2
    ◇ 10 7 6 3                    ◇ J 9 4
    ♣ 10 9 5                      ♣ K 8 6
                    ♠ A J 10 9 5 2
                    ♡ 5
                    ◇ K Q 2
                    ♣ 7 4 3
```

South plays in six spades and West leads ♣ 10. Declarer tries the finesse but East wins and returns a club, won in dummy.

Declarer plays ♠ K and finesses ♠ J, West discarding a heart. Now declarer must somehow avoid losing a trick to East's ♠ Q 8.

His first move is to cash ♡ A and ruff a heart. He follows with three rounds of diamonds, ending in dummy, and ruffs another heart. Then he enters dummy with ♣ J, arriving happily at this position:

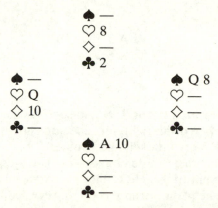

This type of play is known as a *trump coup*. To achieve it, declarer must reduce his trump length to match that of the defender. Sometimes, when declarer is shortening his trumps, he will need to ruff a card that is a winner in its own right. The play is then considered so worthy that it is known as a *grand coup*.

The backwards trump coup

A trump coup may also be possible when the trumps lie over declarer's holding.

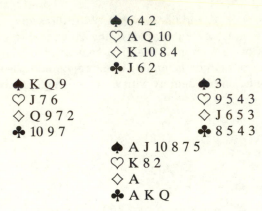

                    ♠ 6 4 2
                    ♡ A Q 10
                    ◇ K 10 8 4
                    ♣ J 6 2

♠ K Q 9   ♠ 3
♡ J 7 6   ♡ 9 5 4 3
◇ Q 9 7 2   ◇ J 6 5 3
♣ 10 9 7   ♣ 8 5 4 3

                    ♠ A J 10 8 7 5
                    ♡ K 8 2
                    ◇ A
                    ♣ A K Q

South opens with a strong 2 ♠ and soon reaches six spades. West, placing ♠ A on his right, sees no reason not to help himself to an extra 50. Very unwisely, he doubles.

Declarer wins the club lead and sees that West must have doubled on trump tricks. He cannot overcome all four trumps with West, so he plans a trump coup to catch K Q x. He must reduce his trumps three times to equal West's length, so three entries will be needed to dummy. He cashes ◇ A and ♣ A K Q, finesses dummy's ♡ 10 successfully (to obtain an extra entry), and ruffs a diamond in hand. He then crosses to dummy twice more in hearts to ruff two more diamonds. When all this passes by without mishap, he is left with only three cards, ♠ A J 10. He exits with ♠ J and West has to return a spade into the tenace. West will need to collect quite a few 50s to balance his account.

Defending against trump coups

While the mechanics of the trump coup are fresh in the mind, we can look at the best way to defend against it. As we have seen, declarer must reach dummy several times to effect a trump coup. He needs enough entries to shorten his trumps and often one more to make the plain-suit lead towards his trump holding.

The defence to a trump coup is therefore double-edged. Firstly, the defenders must refrain from forcing declarer, thereby aiding him to reduce his trumps. Secondly, they must make an early attack on dummy's entries. The defenders made a common mistake on this deal:

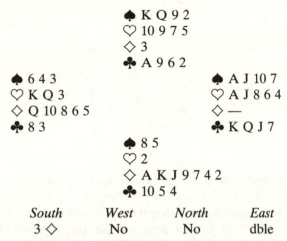

```
                    ♠ K Q 9 2
                    ♡ 10 9 7 5
                    ◇ 3
                    ♣ A 9 6 2
  ♠ 6 4 3                            ♠ A J 10 7
  ♡ K Q 3                            ♡ A J 8 6 4
  ◇ Q 10 8 6 5                       ◇ —
  ♣ 8 3                              ♣ K Q J 7
                    ♠ 8 5
                    ♡ 2
                    ◇ A K J 9 7 4 2
                    ♣ 10 5 4
```

South	West	North	East
3 ◇	No	No	dble

West's prayers were answered when his partner doubled in the fourth seat. He led ♡ K and continued the suit when his partner encouraged. Declarer ruffed, cashed ◇ A, and led a spade to the king and ace. East switched to ♣ K, but the damage was already done. Declarer won in dummy and ruffed another heart, then crossed to ♠ Q and ruffed a spade. When he exited with a club, East won and West was down to his five trumps. On the next trick West had to ruff his partner's club winner and lead a trump into declarer's tenace. Declarer thus escaped for one down.

The defence was misguided. The last thing West should do is force declarer, thereby rendering himself trump-heavy in the end game. If West had led a club, his shortest suit, the defenders would have scored two clubs, two major-suit aces and three trumps, putting declarer three down. Even after a heart lead West could have saved a trick by switching to a spade or a club.

Refusing an overruff

Declarer must sometimes refuse an overruff to preserve his own trump holding. Careless play led to the loss of this contract:

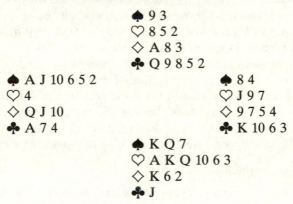

```
                    ♠ J 8 2
                    ♡ Q 6
                    ◇ A K 10 8
                    ♣ 10 8 7 4
♠ A K 10 7 4 3                      ♠ 9 6
♡ 9 7 4 3                           ♡ J
◇ 6 4                               ◇ Q 9 5 2
♣ Q                                 ♣ J 9 6 5 3 2
                    ♠ Q 5
                    ♡ A K 10 8 5 2
                    ◇ J 7 3
                    ♣ A K
```

West cashed two spade honours against four hearts and continued with a third round to kill dummy's jack. East ruffed with ♡ J and declarer saw no harm in overruffing. When the ruff proved to have been from a singleton and the diamond finesse lost, the contract went one down. There was no need to live dangerously. South should have discarded a diamond at trick 3.

Preventing an overruff

Declarer can often prevent an overruff by exchanging a ruff in one suit for a safer ruff in another:

```
                    ♠ 9 3
                    ♡ 8 5 2
                    ◇ A 8 3
                    ♣ Q 9 8 5 2
♠ A J 10 6 5 2                      ♠ 8 4
♡ 4                                 ♡ J 9 7
◇ Q J 10                            ◇ 9 7 5 4
♣ A 7 4                             ♣ K 10 6 3
                    ♠ K Q 7
                    ♡ A K Q 10 6 3
                    ◇ K 6 2
                    ♣ J
```

South plays in four hearts after West has overcalled in spades. West leads ♢ Q and declarer wins in dummy. Nine easy tricks are on view—six trumps in hand, two diamonds and a spade. The tenth will have to come from a ruff in dummy.

Declarer plays a spade to the king and ace and wins the diamond continuation in hand. Since West overcalled in spades, there is quite a risk that the third round of spades will be overruffed. After taking just one round of trumps declarer cashes ♠ Q and leads ♠ 7, throwing dummy's last diamond. His intention is to ruff a diamond instead of a spade. The technique is known as *trading ruffs*.

On this particular hand the defenders have one more shot to play. East also throws a diamond on the third round of spades, and we are left with this position:

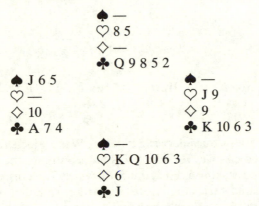

```
                    ♠ —
                    ♡ 8 5
                    ♢ —
                    ♣ Q 9 8 5 2
        ♠ J 6 5                    ♠ —
        ♡ —                        ♡ J 9
        ♢ 10                       ♢ 9
        ♣ A 7 4                    ♣ K 10 6 3
                    ♠ —
                    ♡ K Q 10 6 3
                    ♢ 6
                    ♣ J
```

West cashes ♣ A and continues with ♣ J. If declarer carelessly takes the ruff in hand, East will dispose of his last diamond and be able to overruff the dummy later. Declarer therefore ruffs ♣ J in dummy. If East overruffs, declarer will win and score his diamond ruff. If East does not overruff, declarer will discard his losing diamond immediately.

Trump manoeuvres by the defenders

The defenders also have varied paths to tread in a trump

contract. If the auction has been tentative they should avoid giving away any tricks, adopting a passive defence. When it is evident that declarer has something in hand—or thinks he has—the defenders will lean towards an active defence. This may involve leading from dangerous holdings in an attempt to establish tricks quickly or set up a ruff.

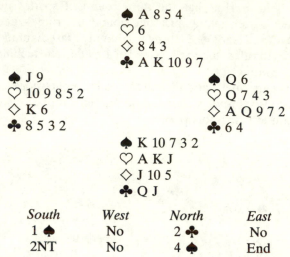

	South	West	North	East
	1 ♠	No	2 ♣	No
	2NT	No	4 ♠	End

In the face of this energetic bidding, West rejects the lead of ♡ 10 as too passive. He leads ◇ K and continues the suit, East winning and cashing a third round, on which West discards a low heart. East now tries the effect of a further round of diamonds, which establishes a fourth trick for the defence. An opening lead of ♡ 10 would have been rather less effective.

When one of the defenders holds length in the trump suit, the general aim of the defence will be to force declarer to ruff and so lose control. This is a typical forcing game:

```
                    ♠ Q 9 4
                    ♡ Q J 2
                    ◇ A J 6 2
                    ♣ A 10 4
  ♠ A 8 7 2                         ♠ 5
  ♡ 8 4                             ♡ 10 9 7 6 3
  ◇ 10 8 7                          ◇ K 9 3
  ♣ K J 7 3                         ♣ Q 8 6 2
                    ♠ K J 10 6 3
                    ♡ A K 5
                    ◇ Q 5 4
                    ♣ 9 5
```

South	West	North	East
		1NT	No
3 ♠	No	4 ♠	End

Holding four trumps, West plans an assault on declarer's trump length. The most promising suit is clubs, so he leads ♣ 3. Declarer ducks the first round and wins the second with dummy's ♣ A. He now plays a trump to the king. If West wins this and forces declarer with a club, the contract will survive. Declarer will take a diamond finesse immediately and dummy's trumps will deal with the fourth round of clubs.

West therefore ducks the first and second round of trumps. Now declarer has no way to turn. Whether he plays next on diamonds or spades, the defenders will be able to strike two more blows at his trump holding and West will eventually score a low trump.

Trump promotions by the defenders

When seeking a trump promotion, it is well known that a defender should refuse to overruff in positions like the following:

$\heartsuit$ K Q J 8

$\heartsuit$ 10 3 $\heartsuit$ A 9 4

$\heartsuit$ 7 6 5 2

West leads a plain suit in which both the dummy and East are void. Dummy ruffs with $\heartsuit$ K and East must on no account overruff. By keeping his powder dry, East ensures two trump tricks. The next position is similar:

$\spadesuit$ 7 4

$\spadesuit$ Q 9 3 $\spadesuit$ K 5

$\spadesuit$ A J 10 8 6 2

If declarer ruffs East's lead of a side suit with $\spadesuit$ J, West must spurn the overruff. Declarer will now lose two trump tricks. On the following hand the position is considerably less obvious:

$\spadesuit$ A K 8
$\heartsuit$ J 7
$\diamondsuit$ Q 9 4 2
$\clubsuit$ K J 9 7

$\spadesuit$ Q 10 5 2 $\spadesuit$ J 9 7 3
$\heartsuit$ 9 5 4 3 $\heartsuit$ Q 10
$\diamondsuit$ 8 5 $\diamondsuit$ A K J 6
$\clubsuit$ A 10 6 $\clubsuit$ 5 4 3

$\spadesuit$ 6 4
$\heartsuit$ A K 8 6 2
$\diamondsuit$ 10 7 3
$\clubsuit$ Q 8 2

South	West	North	East
		1NT	No
2 $\heartsuit$	End		

Hoping to convert a 40 part score, South plays in two hearts and receives the $\diamondsuit$ 8 lead. East takes three rounds of the suit and returns a fourth round, which declarer ruffs with ♡ 8. If West overruffs with ♡ 9, the contract will easily succeed. If West bides his time with a discard, declarer cannot escape two trump losers.

The uppercut

It is often possible for a defender to blast a hole in declarer's trump holding by ruffing high in front of him. This play is picturesquely named the *uppercut*. Here both defenders play a part:

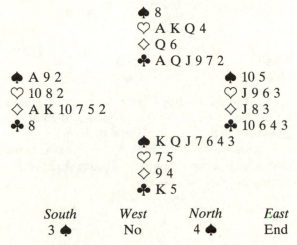

	♠ 8	
	♡ A K Q 4	
	◇ Q 6	
	♣ A Q J 9 7 2	
♠ A 9 2		♠ 10 5
♡ 10 8 2		♡ J 9 6 3
◇ A K 10 7 5 2		◇ J 8 3
♣ 8		♣ 10 6 4 3
	♠ K Q J 7 6 4 3	
	♡ 7 5	
	◇ 9 4	
	♣ K 5	

South	West	North	East
3 ♠	No	4 ♠	End

West begins with ◇ A K and can tell from the play that East has a third diamond. There is no chance of another side winner, so West must aim to promote a second trick in the trump suit. He continues with a third round of diamonds, and when he comes in with ♠ A he leads a fourth diamond. East ruffs with ♠ 10 and West's ♠ 9 becomes the setting trick.

Sometimes a defender can alert a diffident partner to the possibility of an uppercut:

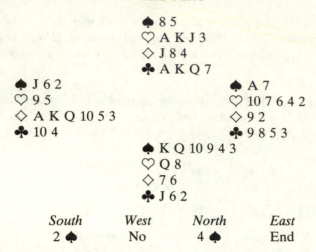

	♠ 8 5	
	♡ A K J 3	
	◇ J 8 4	
	♣ A K Q 7	
♠ J 6 2		♠ A 7
♡ 9 5		♡ 10 7 6 4 2
◇ A K Q 10 5 3		◇ 9 2
♣ 10 4		♣ 9 8 5 3
	♠ K Q 10 9 4 3	
	♡ Q 8	
	◇ 7 6	
	♣ J 6 2	

South	*West*	*North*	*East*
2 ♠	No	4 ♠	End

West leads ◇ A and East drops the 9. West sees the contract will fail if his partner can ruff the third round of diamonds with ♠ A. He continues with ◇ Q and a low diamond.

The pointed underlead of ◇ K makes clear what is required. Realizing that meanness would be out of place, East ruffs with ♠ A, promoting his partner's ♠ J.

17 · Baiting the trap

In the game of poker it is well known that bluffing is a form of advertisement. A few pounds may slip away on the hands where you do bluff, but they return with interest when opponents suspect your genuine bets and invest large sums for the privilege of seeing you.

Although there is certainly a place for bluffing in the bridge auction, it is in the play that most opportunities arise. If the opposition is less than strong, any thick-brushed effort at deception may prove successful. Minor inconsistencies will pass undetected. Against expert opponents, who cast an eagle eye on every spot-card, more subtle brushwork may be needed.

```
                    ♠ K 10 7
                    ♡ A Q 3
                    ◇ 9 6 4
                    ♣ K J 8 4
   ♠ 5 4                          ♠ 8 2
   ♡ J 9 8 6 5 2                  ♡ 10 7
   ◇ K 10 7 3                     ◇ J 8 5 2
   ♣ 2                            ♣ A 10 9 6 3
                    ♠ A Q J 9 6 3
                    ♡ K 4
                    ◇ A Q
                    ♣ Q 7 5
```

South plays in six spades and West leads ♣ 2. From declarer's point of view there is a distinct danger that the lead is a singleton. An inexperienced player might attempt to fool East by throwing his ♣ Q under the ace. This crude effort is unlikely to succeed. East will reason that against a slam his partner would not have led ♣ 2 from a holding of ♣ 7 5 2.

The expert declarer will play ♣ J from dummy at trick 1 and follow with ♣ 7 or ♣ 5 from hand. East may switch to a diamond, thinking that his partner has led from ♣ Q x x.

Scrambling the defenders' signals

One of the most frequent forms of deception is to interfere with the defenders' signalling.

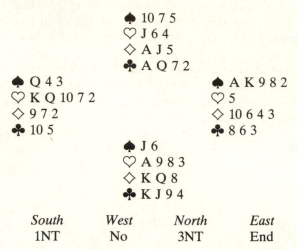

```
                    ♠ 10 7 5
                    ♡ J 6 4
                    ◇ A J 5
                    ♣ A Q 7 2
   ♠ Q 4 3                          ♠ A K 9 8 2
   ♡ K Q 10 7 2                     ♡ 5
   ◇ 9 7 2                          ◇ 10 6 4 3
   ♣ 10 5                           ♣ 8 6 3
                    ♠ J 6
                    ♡ A 9 8 3
                    ◇ K Q 8
                    ♣ K J 9 4
```

South	West	North	East
1NT	No	3NT	End

West leads ♡ K against 3NT. Declarer sees that if he wins the lead and returns a heart towards dummy's knave, West is all too likely to put in the queen and switch to spades. Instead, declarer lets West's ♡ K hold the first trick, contributing ♡ 8 from hand. West may well decide that East's ♡ 5 is an encouraging signal from A 5 3. If he comes to this conclusion and continues with a low heart, declarer will take nine tricks in haste.

The following lay-out occurs frequently:

```
              ♠ 9 6 3
   ♠ A K 10 7              ♠ J 8 4
              ♠ Q 5 2
```

West leads ♠ A against a suit contract. By false-carding from hand, declarer may persuade West to continue the suit may seem to West that East is signalling encouragement fro ♠ Q 4 2 or ♠ 4 2.

When declarer does not want a continuation, he should avoid pointless false cards which may well act against his own interest.

♦ 10 7 2

♦ A K 8 6   ♦ Q 5 4

♦ J 9 3

West leads a side-suit ace against a suit contract, East signalling with ♦ 5. If declarer follows with a 'clever' ♦ 9, West can be sure that his partner's card was an encouraging signal. He will continue the suit. Declarer's best hope is to play ♦ 3 on the first trick. This leaves open the possibility, from West's point of view, that East's ♦ 5 was a discouraging card from ♦ J 9 5.

In most situations, *when declarer wishes to encourage a continuation he should play a high card from hand. To discourage a continuation he should play his lowest card.* In other words he should follow the same signalling method as he would if defending in the East seat.

It is often possible to scramble the defenders' length signals.

```
                    ♠ 8 4 2
                    ♡ 5 3
                    ◇ 8 6 5
                    ♣ K Q J 10 6
♠ K 10 3                              ♠ 9 7 6
♡ J 10 9 7 2                          ♡ 8 6 4
◇ K 3                                 ◇ Q J 9 2
♣ 8 7 4                               ♣ A 9 3
                    ♠ A Q J 5
                    ♡ A K Q
                    ◇ A 10 7 4
                    ♣ 5 2
```

South plays in 3NT and West leads ♡ J, won by the king. If declarer leads ♣ 2 from hand, West will play ♣ 4 (his lowest, showing an odd number) and East will hold up his ace. When declarer leads a second round of clubs from dummy, East will take his ace in the sure knowledge that declarer cannot hold three clubs. Declarer will score three spades, three hearts, a diamond and a club, going one down.

South has played the hand without guile. If he plays ♣ 5 at trick 2 (instead of ♣ 2), East will have a difficult decision when a second round of clubs is led from dummy. From East's point of view, West's ♣ 4 may be the start of an echo from ♣ 4 2. In that case a second hold-up will be imperative.

Feigning weakness in a suit

Particularly in notrump contracts the artful declarer will feign weakness when the defenders attack his stronghold.

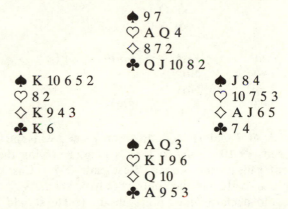

♠ Q 10 6 5
♡ K 5
♢ J 8 2
♣ K J 5 2

♠ K 8 3   ♠ 7 4 2
♡ J 9 6 3 2   ♡ 10 8 7
♢ A 7 6   ♢ K Q 10 4
♣ 10 4   ♣ 9 8 6

♠ A J 9
♡ A Q 4
♢ 9 5 3
♣ A Q 7 3

West leads ♡ 3 against South's 3NT. Declarer sees that all will be well if the spade finesse succeeds. To improve his chances should the finesse fail, declarer wins the first trick with dummy's ♡ K, dropping ♡ Q from hand. When West takes his ♠ K he is likely to continue hearts, placing declarer with an initial holding of ♡ A Q alone.

This little deception is well known but still difficult to counter:

♠ 9 7
♡ A Q 4
♢ 8 7 2
♣ Q J 10 8 2

♠ K 10 6 5 2   ♠ J 8 4
♡ 8 2   ♡ 10 7 5 3
♢ K 9 4 3   ♢ A J 6 5
♣ K 6   ♣ 7 4

♠ A Q 3
♡ K J 9 6
♢ Q 10
♣ A 9 5 3

West leads ♠ 5 against 3NT. Declarer wins East's ♠ J with his ace, hoping that West will place ♠ Q with his partner. Declarer crosses to ♡ A and takes a losing club finesse. There is now an excellent chance that West will continue spades.

Had declarer won the first trick with a mundane ♠ Q, West would have switched to diamonds at high speed. He would have been able to count nine tricks for declarer outside the diamond suit. Declarer's failure to hold up the spade ace is not indicative because the critical play, the club finesse, is into the danger hand, making a hold-up pointless.

Even when the defenders hit declarer's weak spot, an exaggeration of the weakness may induce a faulty defence.

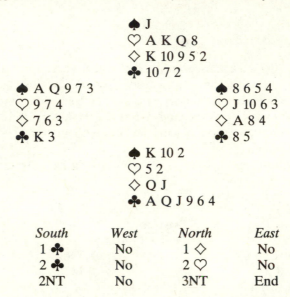

```
                        ♠ J
                        ♡ A K Q 8
                        ◇ K 10 9 5 2
                        ♣ 10 7 2
    ♠ A Q 9 7 3                           ♠ 8 6 5 4
    ♡ 9 7 4                               ♡ J 10 6 3
    ◇ 7 6 3                               ◇ A 8 4
    ♣ K 3                                 ♣ 8 5
                        ♠ K 10 2
                        ♡ 5 2
                        ◇ Q J
                        ♣ A Q J 9 6 4
```

South	West	North	East
1 ♣	No	1 ◇	No
2 ♣	No	2 ♡	No
2NT	No	3NT	End

West leads ♠ 7 against 3NT and dummy's ♠ J wins the trick. Declarer runs ♣ 10, losing to West's king. Knowing that he needs to enter his partner's hand, West leads ◇ 7 to East's ace. Back comes a spade and the contract is two down.

What could declarer have done about it? He should have played his ♠ 10 under dummy's knave at trick 1. West might then place declarer with K 10 doubleton and lay down ♠ A when in with ♣ K.

Deception by the defenders

Declarer's deceptions are not suffered in silence. The defenders will often see a chance to strike back.

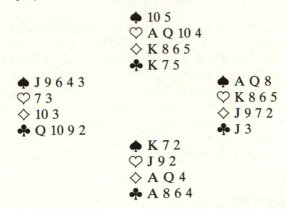

♡ 8 6

♡ J 9 7 2   ♡ A K 5 3

♡ Q 10 4

West leads ♡ 2 against a notrump contract. If East, knowing that declarer cannot hold a doubleton Q x, wins with one of his honours and returns ♡ 3, declarer will probably misguess the suit. This is another *restricted choice* situation. The three holdings, A K x x, A J x x, and K J x x, are equally likely. So, when East wins with a high honour and returns a low card, his remaining honour, if any, is more likely to be the jack.

One important class of deceptive plays is aimed at maintaining a link between the defenders' hands. These so-called communication plays occur frequently.

♠ 10 5
♡ A Q 10 4
◇ K 8 6 5
♣ K 7 5

♠ J 9 6 4 3   ♠ A Q 8
♡ 7 3   ♡ K 8 6 5
◇ 10 3   ◇ J 9 7 2
♣ Q 10 9 2   ♣ J 3

♠ K 7 2
♡ J 9 2
◇ A Q 4
♣ A 8 6 4

West leads ♠ 4 against 3NT. If East wins with ♠ A and returns ♠ Q, declarer will hold up until the third round. When a subsequent heart finesse loses, East will have no spade to return. Declarer scores nine tricks.

At trick 1 East must turn a blind eye to his ♠ A. He must put
on the queen. Declarer can hardly duck, because the lead might
be from A J x x x and the heart finesse might be right. The same
type of play is often right with A J x, also, when the defender
expects declarer to hold K x x rather than Q x x; and even from
A 10 x the 10 may be the winning play. Note, too, a situation
such as:

♡ 5

♡ A 9 7 6 3   ♡ K J 4

♡ Q 10 8 2

The best card for East at trick 1 is the jack.

There are several single-suit situations where a defender must
false-card to give declarer a chance to go wrong.

♠ A J 3

♠ Q 10 4   ♠ 8 7 2

♠ K 9 6 5

Declarer plays a low spade to the jack and then cashes the ace.
If West follows with the 10 on the second round, declarer will
obviously play for the drop on the third round. If West false-
cards ♠ Q on the second round, declarer may place him with an
initial holding of Q 4 alone and take a losing finesse of ♠ 9 on the
third round. West's play of ♠ Q on the second round is an
example of the technique known as *playing the card you are
known to hold*.

West can push declarer off course with the following holding:

♣ A K 10 5

♣ J 9 7 2   ♣ 4

♣ Q 8 6 3

If declarer embarks on this suit by cashing the ace, West
should false-card ♣ 9. This gives declarer the losing option of

continuing with ♣ K, playing East for ♣ J 7 4 2. If West follows low on the first round, declarer is bound to continue with a club to the queen since he cannot pick up ♣ J 9 7 4 with East.

Most players are familiar with:

$$♡ A Q 8 6$$

$$♡ K 7 \qquad\qquad ♡ 10 9 3$$

$$♡ J 5 4 2$$

South plays a low heart to the queen. If East follows with ♡ 3, declarer will continue with ♡ A, picking up the suit without loss. If East plays ♡ 9 on the first round, declarer may play him for ♡ 10 9 and lead ♡ J from hand on the second round.

All three examples we have just seen are known as *obligatory false cards*. If the defender fails to false-card, declarer cannot go wrong. This is another frequently attempted ploy:

$$◇ A J 8 6 3$$

$$◇ Q 7 4 \qquad\qquad ◇ 10 2$$

$$◇ K 9 5$$

When South plays the king from hand East follows with the 10. He hopes that declarer will place him with Q 10 doubleton and play for the drop on the second round. South should generally proceed with the intended finesse. East might play the 10 from Q 10, 10 7, 10 4, 10 2 or single 10, so the odds obviously favour the finesse. An interesting extension of the argument affects declarer's play of this suit:

$$♠ A J 9 7 4$$

$$♠ 10 5 3 \qquad\qquad ♠ Q 6$$

$$♠ K 8 2$$

If East is an opponent who would always false-card with 10 x, declarer should consider playing him for Q x when he follows with a face card at trick 1. At any rate, the expectancies alter

against opponents who, for example, always play the 10 from
10 x or the 9 from 9 x. To prevent declarer benefiting from such
deductions, the defenders should vary their play.

Simulating a desire to ruff

The defenders can sometimes suggest that a ruff is imminent.
Declarer may take evasive action that will prove to his cost.

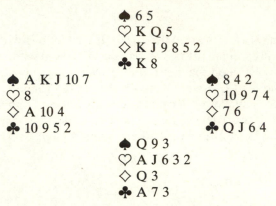

South plays in four hearts after West has overcalled in spades.
West leads two spades and East plays the 8, then the 2,
pretending he holds a doubleton. When West continues with a
third round, declarer is likely to ruff high in the dummy to
prevent East taking a ruff. East will now score a trump trick to
put the contract one down.

Deceptive hold-ups

By pretending that declarer's finesse has succeeded, the
defenders may persuade declarer to misuse his entries. Such
hold-ups are sound only when the suit involved is a critical one in
which the finesse is likely to be repeated.

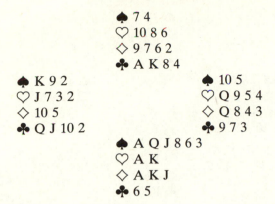

♠ 7 4
♡ 10 8 6
♢ 9 7 6 2
♣ A K 8 4

♠ K 9 2
♡ J 7 3 2
♢ 10 5
♣ Q J 10 2

♠ 10 5
♡ Q 9 5 4
♢ Q 8 4 3
♣ 9 7 3

♠ A Q J 8 6 3
♡ A K
♢ A K J
♣ 6 5

West leads ♣ Q against South's six spade contract. Declarer wins in dummy and plays a trump to the queen. If West wins this trick, declarer will use his remaining entry to dummy to take a successful diamond finesse. Twelve tricks good and true will result.

If West has the imagination to play low when declarer finesses ♠ Q, there is a good chance that declarer will use his second club entry to repeat the spade finesse. Battle-hardened Wests think nothing of holding up with king doubleton. A similar stratagem is to win with a higher card than necessary. This may lead declarer into a losing line of play.

                              ♠ 7 5 4
                              ♡ A 8 5
                              ◇ K 10 9 6 5
                              ♣ A 6

♠ J 9 8 6 3   ♠ K 10 2
♡ 10 7 3   ♡ Q 9 4
◇ 7 4   ◇ A Q 3
♣ 10 7 5   ♣ J 9 4 2

                              ♠ A Q
                              ♡ K J 6 2
                              ◇ J 8 2
                              ♣ K Q 8 3

West leads ♠ 6 against South's 3NT. Declarer wins East's king
with his ace and immediately runs ◇ J. If East wins with ◇ Q
and clears the spade suit, declarer will be forced to play for a
lucky lie in hearts.

To persuade declarer to persist with the diamonds, East
should win the first round of diamonds with his ace. Now, when
the spades are cleared, declarer will surely repeat the diamond
finesse. Note that the play would be equally successful, and twice
as mortifying for declarer, when made from a holding of ◇ A Q
alone.

18 · Turning the screw

No play carries more prestige than the squeeze. It is widely regarded as the expert's hallmark. Although many weird and wonderful squeezes have been discovered, the good news for the aspiring expert is that they rarely occur at the table. Perhaps 90 per cent of all squeezes are variants of the so-called *simple squeeze*. This most important of squeezes is fairly easy to master and extremely rewarding once learnt. We will spend some time on this squeeze before paying homage to its exotic brothers.

The simple squeeze

In this play one defender guards two of the declarer's suits. Declarer cashes a winner in a third suit and the defender has to abandon one of his guards.

Consider this example, played in 7NT on the lead of ♠ J.

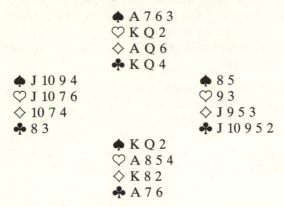

Declarer has twelve top tricks, with an easy thirteenth if either major suit breaks 3–3. If he simply tests the major suits in turn, he will be disappointed. Neither suit breaks.

If he tests just one suit, say the hearts, and then cashes his winners, he will arrive at this position:

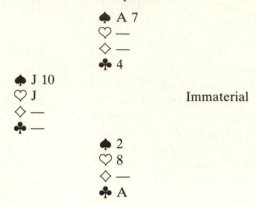

♠ A 7
♡ —
♢ —
♣ 4

♠ J 10
♡ J   Immaterial
♢ —
♣ —

♠ 2
♡ 8
♢ —
♣ A

When declarer plays his ace of clubs, West will be forced to unguard one of the majors.

The simple squeeze we have just seen had three components:

1. The *squeeze card* (♣ A): the card that forced the defender to abandon one of his guards.
2. The *single menace* (♡ 8): a single-card threat, lower in rank than the defender's guard.
3. The *two-card menace* (♠ A 7): a threat accompanied by at least one winner.

These three components are necessary for every simple squeeze. In addition, declarer must be able to gain access to a menace card after it has been unguarded. If this card lies in the same hand as the squeeze card, there is no problem. If it lies in the other hand there must be a way to reach it. This is why a two-card menace is required. Look at this position:

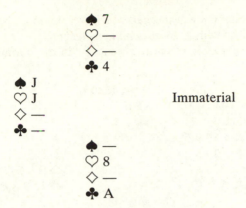

Declarer has two single menaces against West. When he cashes ♣ A, West will throw ♠ J. Dummy's ♠ 7 is now established, but to no purpose. Declarer cannot reach it. Except for a few rare and artificial positions, every squeeze needs a two-card menace.

If we switch the East and West cards in the original hand, the following ending arises:

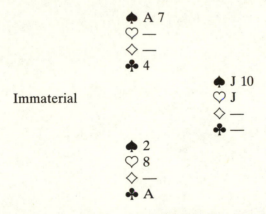

The squeeze is still successful. East must give way to declarer's heart threat or the dummy's spade threat. He cannot hold in one hand the same number of cards that declarer can in two. Such a squeeze, one that will succeed whichever defender holds the two guards, is known as an *automatic squeeze*.

In the next example both threats lie in the dummy:

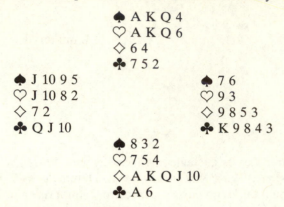

Once more declarer is in 7NT with twelve top tricks. He wins the ♣ Q lead and tests the heart suit, finding that West holds four. Unwilling to rely solely on a 3–3 spade break, he cashes his winners, reaching this position:

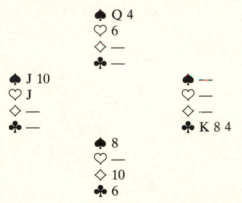

When the squeeze card (♢ 10) is played, West has to discard before the dummy. One extra trick will be made in whichever suit West throws.

Had the two majors been held by East, the squeeze would not have worked, because dummy would have had to discard before the defender with the two guards. This type of squeeze is therefore called a *positional* or *one-way squeeze*. It occurs when the single menace lies in the hand opposite the squeeze card.

Preparing for a squeeze

The two squeezes we have examined required no special preparation. A squeeze operates only when the defender has no spare card to throw when the squeeze card is played. This means that the timing must be right. As a rule, the declarer will be well placed if he can lose at an early stage all the tricks he can afford to lose. Thus if declarer has eight top tricks in 3NT and is hoping to squeeze a ninth, it will usually assist his cause to lose four tricks early on. When the squeeze card is eventually played, the cards of one defender will all be wanted to guard against declarer's threats. All his cards will be *busy*—none can be spared.

If declarer loses, say, only three tricks before playing the squeeze card, the defender will have one spare card, which he may be able to throw without embarrassment. See how this hand develops:

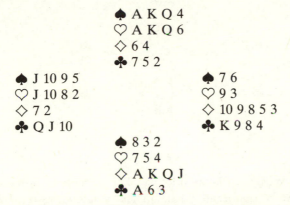

West leads ♣ Q against 6NT. Suppose first that South wins the first trick. He tests the heart suit unsuccessfully, then plays off some winners to arrive at this ending:

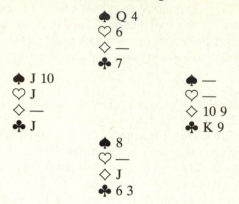

When the squeeze card ($\diamond$ J) is played, West throws $\clubsuit$ J and the squeeze fails. Since declarer could afford to lose one trick, he should have done so at the first opportunity by ducking the first trick. This simple step would have a crucial effect on the end position:

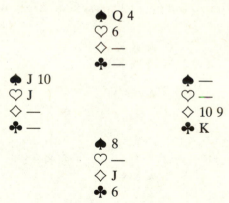

Now West's cards are all busy. This process of tightening up the hand by deliberately losing tricks is known as *rectifying the count*.

Next we shall look at three special manoeuvres that are

sometimes needed to prepare for a squeeze.

Special manoeuvre 1: Isolating the guard

In this play declarer establishes a single menace against one opponent by ruffing out the other opponent's guard in the suit.

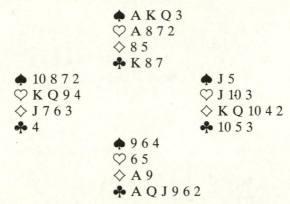

```
                ♠ A K Q 3
                ♡ A 8 7 2
                ◇ 8 5
                ♣ K 8 7
♠ 10 8 7 2                      ♠ J 5
♡ K Q 9 4                      ♡ J 10 3
◇ J 7 6 3                      ◇ K Q 10 4 2
♣ 4                            ♣ 10 5 3
                ♠ 9 6 4
                ♡ 6 5
                ◇ A 9
                ♣ A Q J 9 6 2
```

West leads ♡ K against six clubs. Declarer wins in dummy and draws trumps. He then exits with a low heart, thus rectifying the count. East wins and returns ◇ K, captured by declarer.

If declarer runs the trump suit immediately, no squeeze will materialize since East guards the heart suit as well as West. Instead, declarer crosses to ♠ A and ruffs a low heart in hand. Now only West guards dummy's heart menace. He will be caught in a positional squeeze when the last trump is played.

Special manoeuvre 2: Transferring the menace

```
                        ♠ J 8 2
                        ♡ 9 7 3
                        ◇ A K Q 4
                        ♣ Q 10 2
        ♠ 9 4                           ♠ 7 6 5
        ♡ J 10 6                        ♡ A K Q 2
        ◇ 10 8 5 2                      ◇ J 3
        ♣ J 8 7 4                       ♣ K 9 6 3
                        ♠ A K Q 10 3
                        ♡ 8 5 4
                        ◇ 9 7 6
                        ♣ A 5
```

South	West	North	East
			1NT
2 ♠	No	3 ♠	No
4 ♠	End		

The defenders take three rounds of hearts and switch to a trump, declarer winning and drawing two more rounds. Declarer could rely on a 3–3 diamond break, but he sees an additional chance. There is no hope of squeezing East (whose bid marks him with ♣ K), because he will be discarding after the hand with the threats. Declarer therefore leads ♣ Q from dummy, forcing East to cover. This manoeuvre is known as *transferring the menace*. Now West guards the club suit and the following positional squeeze results:

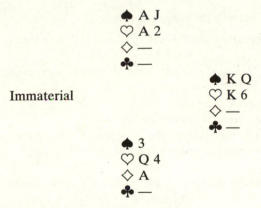

On the last trump West has to unguard one of the minors.

Special manoeuvre 3: The Vienna coup

Consider the following position, in which declarer appears to have the menaces necessary to squeeze East:

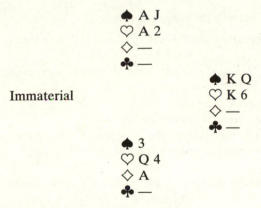

When dummy discards ♡ 2 on the diamond squeeze card, East can afford ♡ 6. Declarer's ♡ Q is established but he cannot reach it. The squeeze fails.

Declarer can overcome this difficulty by cashing ♡ A at an

earlier stage. This unblocking play, in which declarer deliberately sets up a winner in a defender's hand, was identified by a Viennese whist player one gas-lit evening in 1864. After playing this so-called *Vienna Coup*, declarer reaches the following end position:

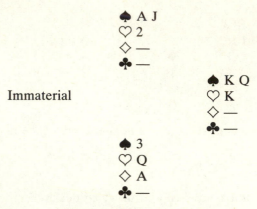

When ♦ A is led, East has no answer.

Summary of playing the simple squeeze

1. Identify the *squeeze card* (usually declarer's last trump or the last card of his main suit).
2. Identify a *two-card menace*, a threat card accompanied by an entry.
3. Identify a *single menace*.
4. *Rectify the count*, if necessary.
5. Consider whether one of these special manoeuvres may be needed: *Isolating the guard*, *Transferring the menace*, *Vienna coup*.
6. Cash the spare winners, ending with the *squeeze card*.

Similar techniques are required in other forms of squeeze. A spectacular form of the simple squeeze, in which both menaces are blocked, is known as the *criss-cross squeeze*.

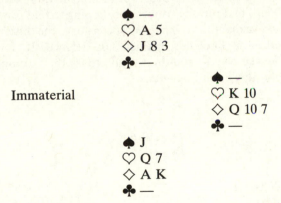

Declarer plays in 7 ♠. He wins the trump lead and draws trumps. He could now cash ◇ A K and play for a positional red-suit squeeze against West. Instead, he gives himself a chance of squeezing *either* opponent by cashing out the black suits. This is the ending:

When ♠ J is led, dummy throws a heart and East has to unguard one of the red suits. Declarer can untangle his tricks now, provided he reads which suit has been bared. A heart lead at trick 1 would have broken the squeeze.

The *trump squeeze* has similar features:

♠ 8 4 3
♡ 9 8 6 2
♢ A K 6 3
♣ A 9

♠ J 10 9 2   ♠ K Q 7 6
♡ 7   ♡ 3
♢ 9 8 5   ♢ Q J 10 2
♣ 10 7 5 3 2   ♣ K Q 8 4

♠ A 5
♡ A K Q J 10 5 4
♢ 7 4
♣ J 6

South	West	North	East
	No	No	1 ♢
4 ♡	No	6 ♡	End

West leads ♠ J and declarer ducks to rectify the count. West continues with a spade to the ace. Declarer might now cash ♣ A (Vienna Coup) and run the trump suit, hoping to find East with ♣ K Q and five diamonds. Since West can guard the third round of diamonds, this line fails against best defence. If, instead, declarer leaves ♣ A standing and runs the trump suit immediately, this ending results:

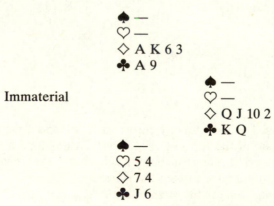

♠ —
♡ —
♢ A K 6 3
♣ A 9

Immaterial

♠ —
♡ —
♢ Q J 10 2
♣ K Q

♠ —
♡ 5 4
♢ 7 4
♣ J 6

On the penultimate trump dummy throws ♣ 9 and East is squeezed. This end position shows the two elements of a trump squeeze—a blocked threat in the same hand as the last trump, and in the other hand a threat that can be established by ruffing. On this occasion the squeeze could have been broken up by a switch to clubs at trick 2.

Finally, here is a *double squeeze*, where both opponents are under pressure:

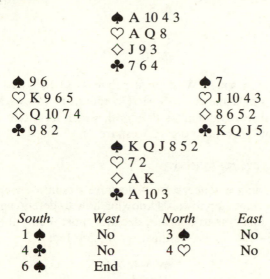

South	West	North	East
1 ♠	No	3 ♠	No
4 ♣	No	4 ♡	No
6 ♠	End		

An ambitious auction carries South to 6 ♠. West leads ♣ 9 and declarer ducks East's jack to rectify the count. East switches to a diamond, which declarer wins in hand. He now runs the trump suit to produce this ending:

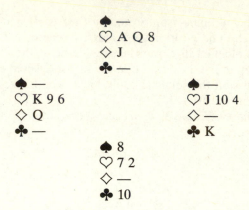

On the last spade West must retain $\diamond$ Q to guard against dummy's single menace ($\diamond$ J). He therefore throws a heart. Declarer discards dummy's diamond, which has done yeoman service, and East has no card to spare.

Defending against squeezes

Understanding a squeeze from declarer's point of view is the most important step towards knowing how to defend against it. For most squeezes to operate, declarer must rectify the count. Very well—the defenders must try to stop him.

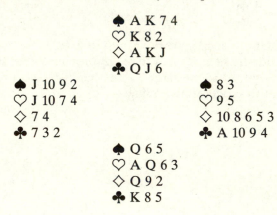

South	*West*	*North*	*East*
1NT	No	6NT	End

Declarer wins the spade lead and plays a club to the queen. If East takes this trick, or the next round of clubs, declarer will have an easy squeeze against West in the majors. If East can steel himself to duck twice, the slam cannot be made. West will have a spare card to play (his third club) when the last diamond is cashed. To hold up twice would cost a trick if South held ♣ K x x x, but partner's ♣ 2 precludes this possibility.

The defenders can often avert an impending squeeze by destroying one of declarer's menaces.

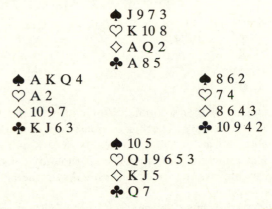

West cashes two top spades against four hearts, his partner playing upwards. If West switches to diamonds now, declarer will eventually squeeze him in the black suits.

West can avoid this gory fate by continuing with ♠ Q at trick 3. Declarer will ruff and try to slip through the jack of trumps. West will have none of this, of course. He will rise with the ace and lead a fourth round of spades to kill declarer's spade menace.

In our last example of squeeze defence, the defenders attack declarer's two-card menace.

```
                            ♠ Q 10 6
                            ♡ A 8 5
                            ◇ Q 8 6 5
                            ♣ J 9 2
      ♠ 8                                          ♠ 4
      ♡ K J 4 2                                    ♡ 10 9 7 3
      ◇ J 10 3                                     ◇ A K 9 7 2
      ♣ Q 8 6 4 3                                  ♣ 10 7 5
                            ♠ A K J 9 7 5 3 2
                            ♡ Q 6
                            ◇ 4
                            ♣ A K
```

South	West	North	East
2 ♣	No	2NT	No
3 ♠	No	4 ♡	No
4NT	No	5 ◇	dble
6 ♠	End		

Respecting his partner's double, West leads ◇ J and declarer plays low in the dummy. There is obviously only one diamond trick available, so East overtakes the lead with ◇ K and switches to ♡ 10. This attack on dummy's ♡ A is the only constructive defence available. As the cards lie, it breaks up the heart-club squeeze on West.

Opponents who have executed a successful squeeze will contest the next few hands with added confidence and vigour. All the more reason to rob them of their moment of glory with a well timed hold-up or switch. You can always give them a friendly smile afterwards; or a disdainful look, if that is your nature.